D0246423

IT MUST
NEVER HAPPEN
AGAIN

XB00 000008 1054

IT MUST NEVER HAPPEN AGAIN

THE LESSONS LEARNED FROM THE SHORT LIFE AND TERRIBLE DEATH OF BABY P

JOHN McSHANE

JOHN BLAKE

WOLVERHAMPTON PUBLIC LIBRARIES	
XB000000081054	
Bertrams	08/11/2010
362.7609MC	£7.99
SV	01165592

Published by John Blake Publishing Ltd,
3 Bramber Court, 2 Bramber Road,
London W14 9PB, England

www.blake.co.uk

First published in paperback in 2009

ISBN 978 1 84454 789 0

All rights reserved. No part of this publication may be reproduced, stored in a
retrieval system, or in any form or by any means, without the prior permission
in writing of the publisher, nor be otherwise circulated in any form of binding
or cover other than that in which it is published and without a similar
condition including this condition being imposed on the subsequent publisher.

British Library Cataloguing-in-Publication Data:
A catalogue record for this book is available from the British Library.

Design by www.envydesign.co.uk

Printed and bound in Great Britain by CPI Bookmarque, Croydon CR0 4TD

1 3 5 7 9 10 8 6 4 2

© Text copyright John McShane 2009

Papers used by John Blake Publishing are natural, recyclable products made
from wood grown in sustainable forests. The manufacturing processes conform
to the environmental regulations of the country of origin.

Every attempt has been made to contact the relevant copyright-holders,
but some were unobtainable. We would be grateful if the
appropriate people could contact us.

CONTENTS

Prologue   vii

1   Wednesday's Child   1

2   Evil Arrives   15

3   A Catalogue of Neglect   23

4   House of Horror   49

5   Running From Justice   65

6   Failings & Recriminations   75

7   The Whistleblower   97

8   More Horrors Emerge   107

9   The Report   127

10   Changes   155

11   It Must Never Happen Again   167

12   Further Abuse   205

13   The Trial   223

14   Named & Shamed   237

Personnel involved in the Baby P case   249

Timetable of events   251

PROLOGUE

N O ONE deserved to die in such a way, in surroundings like that.

Dog and human excrement littered the floor of the run-down four-bedroom house in a shabby part of north London. Dead rats and chickens were lying about, destined to be fed to two pet snakes and the pack of vicious dogs living in the building. On the kitchen sideboard, a dismembered rabbit was beginning to rot. The house was infested with fleas and there was a large collection of knives, martial art weapons and Nazi memorabilia.

There was also a bloodstained cot. Inside lay a child, a dead child; a child who, during his achingly short life, was forced to scavenge food from other youngsters and even tried to eat dirt from the garden. He was a child with curling, cornfield-blond hair, who once had angel-innocent eyes – a look that somehow made what happened to him in the short time that he lived on Earth seem even worse. Regardless of appearance, no child should suffer as he did, yet somehow the purity of his tiny face made the torment he went through seem even more appalling.

This was a child who, in the 17 months that he had been alive, had been dealt with by a succession of health professionals from many walks of life – social workers, doctors, lawyers and police. Some 60 times in all, those whose role in life it was to protect the vulnerable came into and out of his life, but it made no difference. The 23lb boy was even on the local council's Child Protection Register, a phrase that now seems so inappropriate as to be grotesque. The list of his injuries appeared endless, but included a spine broken 'like a hinge' with the level of force usually suffered by victims of a car crash and eight broken ribs – neither were spotted by the doctor who examined him just days earlier. In his stomach was one of his own tiny teeth, placed there by a punch from a brute of a man who knocked it out of his little jaw and down his throat. A finger and toenail had been torn off, his body was infested with lice and his face and ears bruised and cut. There were marks in his scalp that could well have been made by a dog's teeth.

The 999 call summoning an ambulence to his home was made at 11.36 am, on 3 August 2007. They arrived within minutes, only to find the child's body already stiff and blue. His beautiful hair had been shorn. The paramedics were in the house a mere three minutes and were eager to rush the boy to hospital. Even so, the child's mother asked them not to be so hasty, to take their time. Her reason? She didn't want to leave without her cigarettes. At 11.49 the ambulance reached North Middlesex University Hospital in Edmonton, London, only for the inevitable pronouncement to be made at 12.19. It was the same hospital in which he had been born and now the circle was complete. Later that afternoon the child's 27-year-old mother was arrested and 11 days after that, two men who had been living with her at her home were also charged.

Their subsequent trial and convictions and the detail that emerged were, in the words of that old cliché, 'to shock the nation'. Even in a country that, with every passing day was apparently losing the ability to have its passions aroused, there was horror. Every new revelation of the very hell of the child's existence and the behaviour, either deliberately cruel on the part of the adult monsters around him or staggeringly inept when it came to those professionals tasked with his care and wellbeing, led to the inevitable questions being posed: how had it happened? What had gone wrong with the system that allowed a child under the protection of, supposedly, one of the most advanced, humane societies in the world to suffer and die so? How many more might endure his fate and how many mistakes would be made by those around them? What exactly took place in the short, sad time that the boy lived in the house where he died, the 'home' that was to form the backdrop for so much suffering and depravity? How could any human being cause a child to suffer in the way that he had?

This is the story of that poor child, the doomed youngster with the 'help-me' eyes. The boy's real name was Peter Connelly but he will always be known as 'Baby P'.

1

WEDNESDAY'S
CHILD

IT WAS the Victorians who changed the shape of Britain forever. A combination of the railway age and the rapidity of mass house-building that ensued turned once-green pastures into the urban sprawl we recognise today in our large cities and towns. Tottenham, north London, where poor, doomed Baby P lived and died, is a perfect example of such change.

The Romans built Ermine Street to take their troops and traders to Lincoln and on to York, through what was to become Tottenham. That route would evolve into the A10, now clogged with traffic moving slowly in and out of London, much of it travelling bumper-to-bumper, at speeds slower than the Romans managed some 2,000 years earlier.

There was a settlement, albeit a small one, in the area over 1,000 years ago. Its modern name is believed to have derived from those days: in medieval times Tota, a local farmer, occupied a hamlet there and 'Tota's Hamlet', as it was known, was mentioned in its by-then truncated form as 'Toteham' in the eleventh-century Domesday Book. Eventually, this transformed into the modern 'Tottenham'.

By the 1700s a few large houses had been built in the area, which was largely still open fields, enabling their affluent owners to enjoy the pleasures of the countryside, yet still be within striking distance of bustling London, six miles away.

But the Victorian era brought an end to all that, as the rural idyll disappeared altogether with the expansion of the railways. The introduction of cheap workmen's fares on the trains in the 1870s meant the upper- and middle-class homes were soon swamped by road after road of cheaper houses for the less prosperous, who could now get into London at minimal cost. So it was that 'modern', recognisable and definitely very working-class Tottenham was born. Each decade, the population of the area doubled – an astonishing rate of increase – and by 1891, it stood at almost 100,000.

Some of the first bombs that were to fall on London during World War II landed on Tottenham and Hitler's last roll of the dice, the V1 and V2 pilotless bombs, also hit the area. The district achieved further notoriety in 1985, when PC Keith Blakelock, a 40-year-old father of three, was killed by a mob during a riot on the area's massive Broadwater Farm estate when he was surrounded by masked and balaclava-wearing rioters armed with sticks, knives and machetes, who mercilessly hacked him to death.

Throughout its more recent history there has also been an automatic, and far less violent, link with another name synonymous with the area: Tottenham Hotspur Football Club.

For more than a century, the team has played at the famous White Hart Lane on the High Street, the successor to the old Roman road.

In the mid-1960s came a change far less dramatic than wars or riots, far less joyful than the triumphs of the area's beloved Spurs, at that time enjoying the most successful spell in their history. It was an occurrence that the majority of those affected by it probably cared little for, or showed scant interest in.

The London Borough of Haringey was formed in 1965 by the amalgamation of the Borough Councils of Hornsey, Tottenham and Wood Green, under the London Local Government Act of 1963, which was aimed at reducing the number of local government areas in the capital. The Act meant that affluent Highgate, Muswell Hill and Crouch End with their elegant houses – soon to experience ever-increasing prices, bringing with it the essential gentrification accessories of smart restaurants and articulate, upwardly-mobile young professionals, in the west of the new area were under the same administration as the far less prosperous and by now run-down Tottenham and Wood Green districts to the east.

'Local Government Reorganisation' is hardly a topic to set pulses racing. Most people simply want their household waste to be regularly collected, their streets constantly cleaned, good schools for their children and a wide range of civic amenities to enjoy, so the name or the structure of the organisation providing them is almost irrelevant – until, of course, something goes wrong.

But that dull, administrative change in the midst of all the social upheaval and excitement that was the sixties was to have an effect on the events that were to unfold around Baby P and those involved with him.

By the time he was born, in 2006, Haringey's 11 square miles was home to a population that, at a conservative estimate, numbered almost a quarter of a million. Over a third of those living there came from ethnic minority backgrounds. Indeed, part of Tottenham was considered the most ethnically diverse area in Western Europe.

According to the 2001 Census, the largest groups were: Caribbean 11%; African 10%; Asian (Indian, Pakistani and Bangladeshi) 8%; Eastern European, Turkish and Kurdish 5% and Irish 4%. No doubt those figures will have changed in the years since the Census was conducted as more people from Eastern Europe and virtually every country in the world flooded in on a daily basis. Many would be known to what is still somewhat quaintly referred to as, 'the authorities' – a great many more, meanwhile, would remain unknown.

Almost half the pupils in Haringey schools still regard English as their second language and one estimate is that almost 200 languages are spoken every day in the area. Many of the businesses are family-run or small by today's standards, but local unemployment remains far higher than the national average. The Borough of Haringey has a population and budget far larger than some nations and in today's Britain that means a massive bureaucratic administration is needed to run the area.

This was the crowded, chaotic society that Baby P was born into.

When he first saw the light of day in 2006, no one could predict that Peter Connelly would eventually take his place in the list of a lost generation of children whose lives would tragically end in brutality and hate although, as we will later see, the omens were depressingly bad given the background of the adults who were to surround him in the coming months.

Peter was born on Wednesday, 1 March 2006, and as if to fulfil the prophecy in the traditional children's nursery rhyme, this Wednesday's child certainly was 'full of woe'. He came into the world at the North Middlesex University Hospital, an institution whose very name conjures up an image of academics, leafy lanes and green fields, although the reality is far from some intellectual, country idyll. Caring for the inhabitants in the surrounding Haringey and Enfield, it is a massive structure along the southern side of the North Circular Road, where drivers stuck in the inevitable traffic-jams, both east and west, have for decades gazed disinterestedly at its post-war ugliness.

Even by hospital standards, it is a depressing building, much of it a combination of concrete and glass that at first glance almost exudes an air of Eastern-Bloc harshness. Perhaps it is no coincidence that its history dates back to the establishment on the site of a workhouse in the early days of Queen Victoria's reign, which gradually evolved – by 1910 – into a hospital that, by the time Peter Connelly was born, treated over 46,000 inpatients and about 200,000 outpatients, as well as 157,000 people in the Accident and Emergency and Walk-in Centres, annually. With 420 beds and over 2,000 staff it was, and remains, a major provider of healthcare in the area. One of those cared for by the hospital was Tracey Connelly, Peter's mother.

Like doomed Peter himself, for a large period of the horror

story about to unfold, her name could not be made public. Indeed, it wasn't until over two years after her son's death and the lifting of the legal restrictions that had been put in place, that the world at large knew full details – not just of her name, but the life she had led. Her anonymity, and that of her son, was both a legal and moral necessity to protect the innocent who had become involved through no wish of their own in her life and the lives of the two men to share her shame. That secrecy was only superficial, however, as those connected with Peter's death, including the boy himself, had already been named in a variety of places, ranging from foreign newspapers to countless internet references, including MySpace, Facebook and Bebo. Over one million joined social networking pages which identified them and their names were sent by viral text to thousands of mobile phone users at a time when legally, they should not have been identified.

Not all the 'naming and shaming' was so hi-tech, though – there were even posters with their photographs taped onto trees and lamp-posts in Tottenham within days of the arrests, like some throwback to the 'wanted' posters once hammered in place on wooden walls in the Wild West. Under the headline, JUSTICE FOR BABY P, the posters described Tracey Connelly as 'a vile woman' and named the men involved with her, proclaiming, THEY DESERVE TO DIE! But it must be pointed out that even now, with her identity known, there are still other innocent parties or victims involved, directly or indirectly with the events in that terrible household, who cannot be named or identified, who must remain anonymous in this book.

Bearing those restrictions in mind, it is still possible to

examine the background of Tracey Connelly, the very antithesis of the image that the word 'mother' conjures up, a woman who spent the time that she should have been caring for Peter and his sisters drinking heavily, chain-smoking and constantly watching porn and television poker.

So what had turned Tracey Connelly into a monster seemingly devoid of any virtues whatsoever, whose image and name will be forever synonymous with cruelty and amorality?

The details of the case to subsequently emerge in no way justify her actions – or indeed *lack* of them – towards her son, nothing can do that, but they go a long way towards explaining her character and subsequent attitude to life, her behaviour and how all this would impact on her handsome young son. The facts paint a depressing picture of an underclass automatically passing on an inheritance of low-expectation, total reliance on the State for both financial and moral support and an inevitability of failure, hopelessness and dysfunction that is hard to deny. With it goes an unspoken 'taken' that the State – in the form of 'Social Services' or 'the Council' – will also act in a parental role, taking over the responsibilities that in other, more caring sectors of society belong to parents.

Tracey Connelly's own mother is a perfect illustration of how this baton of despair can be handed from one generation to the other. Mary O'Connor – 'Nula' to those who know her – is the first to admit, in a masterpiece of understatement, that she has had, 'a hard, hard life.' Born in Ireland, she was just four days old when her mother died and although her father remarried, her stepmother died when she was only five. O'Connor once admitted that she and her father, a former army man who had been raised in an orphanage, 'never connected' apart from when he was drunk. As a young girl, she was so frightened of him that she frequently wet herself in fear and he would regularly beat her.

At the age of nine she became the victim of sexual molestation by a relative and at 13, she stabbed a girl with a pair of scissors. O'Connor was then placed in a convent home, remarking later that it was either that or prostitution, and in her early 20s she came to Britain, where she briefly married a fork-lift truck driver before separating and marrying Football Pools salesman Garry Cox in Leicester.

Cox managed to secure them a council flat but he was also the type of man who would not permit his partner to venture from the home without his permission. If his wife went out shopping, he would time her to make sure that she returned home inside what he thought was the proper time and he also subjected her to regular beatings. She was used to that, though – this was, after all, the life she had been born into – and so she regarded his actions as nothing extraordinary. Eventually, she could take no more and so she stabbed her husband – who she classified a sadist – in the stomach with a knife, subsequently receiving two years' probation for her crime. It's hardly surprising that she was unfaithful during the marriage, although she disputes the version of events by which she is said to have conceived her daughter.

O'Connor and Cox had a son and four years later, on 29 June 1981, Tracey Connelly was born in Leicester. She lived there for three years until her mother and Cox – who Tracey had always regarded as her natural father throughout childhood –

separated. From the start, Cox took to calling Tracey 'the bastard', for reasons that will soon become clear. Her parents' relationship had been a stormy one and both she and her brother witnessed the domestic violence that took place. Cox would punch his wife with his fists on a daily basis, blaming her for the squalor in which they lived and telling their children that she was 'evil'. On one occasion he hit her so savagely that the pet dog fled the room in terror. The couple eventually split and, in 1988, Garry Cox died unexpectedly from a heart attack.

The family had moved to Islington but Tracey's brother had difficulties settling in and his behaviour was later described as 'challenging'. Alongside all the mayhem, Connelly's childhood – which she herself would later describe as 'shitty' – continued unabated and she frequently wore ripped and dirty clothes (one of her nicknames was 'Tracey the Tramp').

At school in London she would arrive wearing old tracksuit bottoms and ripped trainers. Overweight and dirty, she was the classic kid that no one wanted to play with and as a result of this, she would be beaten up. One visitor to the family home noticed dog excrement on the floor and no sheets on the beds, a squalid image that was to be mirrored in Tracey's adult life. On another occasion a visitor saw the young girl pick up a carpet tile covered in dog excrement from their black mongrel, drop the offending matter in a bin inside the house, then calmly replace the tile.

In later years, Tracey Connelly would also state that she was raped on more than one occasion by a male relative. It all fitted in. Visitors to the flat would often see her emaciated mother in bed with a boyfriend, smoking cannabis. At the tender age of 11,

Connelly herself would venture up dark alleyways with older boys.

She was then given the news that no girl on the threshold of womanhood wishes to hear – that Garry Cox was not, contrary to what she had believed for years, her natural father. Instead he had watched while another man had sex with his wife. Convicted rapist Richard Johnson later said that the heavy-drinking Cox, who also smoked cannabis on a regular basis, paid him £5 to sleep with O'Connor as part of a joke. Even Johnson, who would later appear in Baby P's life, was to admit, 'It was the biggest regret of my life.' As well as taking drugs, by her own admission O'Connor admits that she 'liked a good drink when I had money' and although she disputes this version of events, she does say that she had an affair with him.

Exactly what happened may never be known, but Connelly later claimed that the revelation that she was, in fact, Johnson's child, 'drove her wild' for a spell although by then the authorities were already getting involved with her family.

His mother described how she told her son that he was going to go with her to get some new trainers, only for her to march him off to Social Services instead, saying that once they tired of him, they could return him to her. When the boy was eventually returned to his mother, she asked for a new cooker as well in some bizarre form of what she felt in her mind was compensation for allowing her own child back home.

In 1991, the boy's sister was also placed on the Register, this time under the category of 'neglect'. Even at this tender age there were concerns, over both her appearance and her hygiene. Years later, an official report was to state: 'the parenting she received was inconsistent and there is evidence that it was abusive.' Certainly, this was the early part of a cycle of deprivation that would only repeat itself as time went by.

In June of 1992, Connelly was removed from the Child Protection Register and referred to Child Guidance. It was thought that she needed to be in 'a special educational setting' and the following year, she attended what Islington Council somewhat inappropriately referred to as a 'boarding school'. This was not the establishment such as the name usually signifies: Farney Close School, near Haywards Heath in West Sussex, specialised in dealing with children with emotional and social problems.

Perhaps this was the chance for her to escape the inevitability of the underclass life for which she seemed destined – after all, the school had helped Daley Thompson as a small boy and he had gone on to become an Olympic gold medal winner and arguably the greatest decathlete in history. Indeed, he himself had spoken in praise of the school, as had many others, including official inspectors. But if this was her chance, then she let it slip. Surrounded by many other troubled teenagers, Connelly – described as 'very moody and promiscuous' – would kiss other girls in her class to grab the attention of her peers. She was also given a new nickname: 'Stig' – a word used to describe someone with poor dress-sense from a lowly background. A longer version was even more unpleasant – 'Stig of the Dump'.

While at Farney Close she would shower only once a week and her face was covered in spots. Chain-smoking Connelly used to wear Doc Martens because her size-10 feet were too large for girls' shoes. She had a bad temper and frequently got into fights. Her mother has said that despite her young daughter's size, she was still the subject of bullying. No one came to visit her at the Sussex school and during her time there, while on visits to London, there were suggestions that she resorted to prostitution to earn money.

Also, disturbingly, a relative of Connelly's was involved in the Islington childcare scandal of the time, in which there was widespread abuse of youngsters in Council care. That particular episode is worthy of greater space than can be devoted to it here, however, but the link with what would occur years later in Tottenham cannot be dismissed. Already the infamous 'cycle of abuse' was in progress.

While this sordid story unravelled itself, an equally disturbing event took place in 1995, some 60 miles away in Whitstable, known as the 'Pearl of Kent' because of its long association with the oyster trade. The charming seaside town was becoming popular with a young and fashionable crowd from London, who bought homes there or visited at weekends. Worlds away from the colour supplement lifestyle, however, an elderly local woman was assaulted in her own home by two young brothers. Wearing Guy Fawkes' masks, the pair beat up 82-year-old Hilda Barker and locked her in a wardrobe in an attempt to make her change her will. She was so traumatised by the ordeal – reported by a female member of her family – that she had to be taken into care. Her attackers were questioned and charged, but the case never reached court because of 'lack of admissible evidence'. Soon afterwards, she died of pneumonia and the case was subsequently dropped. Whenever the young men had previously called on her over a period of several months, the pensioner had been terrified. Neighbours recalled that she was black and blue after their visits. Steven Barker and his elder brother Jason were the young men who frightened and tortured her: they were her grandsons.

Years later, the paths of the two young men would cross with Connelly, but by the mid-1990s, her education was coming to an end. The travesty of a childhood now over, she left school at 15, with GCSEs in English and IT, and briefly worked as a hairdresser as well as in a bar. However, her life was to change dramatically for she was about to meet the man who would become her husband and father to her children.

After all, as Connelly once told a friend, all she ever really wanted was, 'a houseful of kids.'

2

EVIL ARRIVES

TRACEY CONNELLY was 16 when she met the man who was to become her husband (and cannot be named for legal reasons). He was older than her and was in full-time employment. This was not, of course, going to be a fairytale marriage, how could it be? Instead, this was to be a familiar cycle of pregnancies, affairs, marital break-up, drink and 'the boyfriend' moving in.

The reaction of Connelly's mother to his arrival on the scene hardly boded well:

'I didn't think much of him,' Mary O'Connor was to say 'and I still don't. But he was a good provider. She had everything within reason. He did three shifts and he cooked, cleaned and washed her clothes. He even gave her a lovely home, even though she got it through the council. And he wasn't violent or anything like that.' By the standards of the life she had lived and the life she was about to lead, the non-violence of the new man in Tracey's life was at least one plus in the relationship that was to follow.

Connelly soon became pregnant and the couple moved into a rented, funded flat before their first daughter was born. Another daughter followed, after which she was treated for post-natal depression, and then in July 2003, by which time they had moved to a larger home, she married the father of the two girls at Haringey Civic Centre, a modern building just to the north of the bustling Wood Green shopping centre.

Connelly wore a strange patterned, purple bodice wedding dress and long white veil, while her husband had on a dark red shirt with a white tie when they signed the register. Later she said that she had only got married because she was under pressure from her mother-in-law, hardly a great reason.

Her wedding pictures show her with a glass of her favourite vodka and Coke in hand, singing a karaoke version of one of her favourite songs, Sonny and Cher's, 'I Got You Babe'. One guest at the wedding recalls the occasion as being 'quite a happy affair' after which a handful of people went back to the couple's home following the reception at a Tottenham pub. But the guest, a neighbour and friend of the duo, also noticed warning signs: Connelly would go out on her own, wearing low-cut tops and short dresses and drink heavily in local pubs.

A third girl was to follow and it was around this time that Connelly also made contact with her biological father, who then started to become a regular visitor to his daughter's home. Again, she described herself as being depressed after giving birth and also said that her husband's shift-work played a part in her feeling down. Their home in Tottenham was cramped and untidy and visitors noticed a smell of urine.

The marriage was not a happy one and less than three months

after the wedding ceremony, Tracey kicked her husband out of their home amid rumours that she was having an affair with one of his friends. The couple reconciled, but by the time of Peter's birth in March 2006 the marriage was, to all intents and purposes, over. That summer, with Connelly again depressed, Peter's father moved out. The reason: in June of that year a new man who Tracey had met when he carried out repairs at her home had come into her life. He was an odd-job man, who carried out occasional work – his name was Steven Barker.

Barker on his own would have been bad enough for little Peter, but he also had an elder brother Jason, who was definitely a rotten apple from the same tree.

Steven Barker was 6ft 4in tall and weighed in at around 18 stone. It was hardly a surprise that his arrival on the scene heralded the end of the marriage; he would be lying on the sofa, waiting for his meal to be served when Peter's father returned home from work.

So what sort of man was Steven Barker and how had he grown into the monster that he undoubtedly became?

Part of the answer seemed to be that – if there is such a thing as genuine evil in a child – he might well have been that malevolent force. From an early age he had shown a streak of cruelty that was to continually emerge throughout later years.

As a youngster he delighted in tormenting guinea pigs and skinning frogs alive. Then, just to complete the 'game', he would tear their legs off.

When he was young, he had been given the nickname 'Fatboy' and suffered bullying in his teens – as did Connelly. One of the consequences of bullying is that quite often the victim turns into the perpetrator in later life, and that is exactly what happened with Steven Barker. Eventually he was sent to live with relatives on a tough estate in Tottenham and he was even, for a spell, dubbed 'BFG' after the Big Friendly Giant in the Roald Dahl children's story. But his problems continued, so much so that he was eventually sent to the nearby Moselle special needs school. The school describes itself as 'a co-educational day special school for up to 131 learners with special educational needs' and in recent years an Ofsted inspection decided: 'This is an outstanding school. Leadership and management are outstanding and pupil achievement is at the heart of all decision making. Given their starting points, and the severe barriers to learning, the achievements of a great majority of pupils are outstanding. Pupils' outstanding progress in their personal development is due to the excellent relationships, teaching, team-work, care, support and guidance they receive for the individual needs. There is a strong emphasis on including all pupils in all aspects of school life and there are opportunities for pupils to work alongside their mainstream peers.'

Sadly, in spite of all the good work it undoubtedly has done, Steven Barker was not to be one of the success stories of the school, tucked away in a street not too far from the Broadwater Farm Estate.

Paradoxically, some people remember that as a youngster Steven could also be quite pleasant, but then his elder brother Jason appeared on the scene. Jason had a penchant – if that is not too kind a word to use – for young girls, quite often underage. When their brothers or other male relatives found out about his activities, he would seek out the protection of his large, younger sibling.

One of the youths from the area recalled: 'Steven was really slow, but he never caused any trouble. We called him the "BFG". But if you told him to do something, he would do it; that was always the danger with him, he was easily led. When Jason showed up, he started getting him into trouble. Although Steven never started anything, once Jason got him involved, he would get totally involved. He would do anything Jason told him to. He was brainwashed by him, completely under his spell.'

Steven had an IQ of just 60, yet he was actually regarded as one of the brightest children at the special school, although when he left there was no chance of him moving on to further education so he started working as a labourer and odd-job man.

By the time he reached his twenties, he had started to develop a new fascination, this time with everything military. And there was one famous armed force that he became besotted with, Hitler's Nazi troops. Soon he began spending what money he had on war memorabilia, such as knives and replica guns. He would walk the streets of Wood Green and Tottenham in a camouflage jacket, wearing thick-soled, strap-on army boots.

Often he would visit local tattoo parlours and, after careful perusal of the 'menu', invariably plump for a design that in some way was linked to the Nazi era. In his spare time – and he had an awful lot of that – he would watch videos of one of his heroes, Adolf Hitler.

And so it was that in June 2006, while he was carrying out repairs for a property agency, that he met Tracey Connelly. By now she was bored with her older husband and he himself reached breaking point when Connelly decided to take her new man to a school reunion rather than go accompanied by the father of her children. A month later, Peter's father packed his bags and left. By November 2006, Barker moved in with Connelly. She was so besotted that she had his initials 'S.R.B.' tattooed in black ink on her shoulder and eagerly told those who cared to listen that she had met 'every girl's dream.' In one e-mail to a friend she said, 'My fella is nuts, but being in love is great.'

By early 2007 the family had moved to Penshurst Road, a four-bedroom house funded by benefit payments of approximately £400 a week, and in June of that year, brother Jason arrived on the doorstep with his girlfriend. By the very nature of the lives they all led, it should come as no surprise to learn that she was just 15 years old. It was hardly a happy home that this couple had arrived at – Barker and Connelly's romance was already cooling; their sex life had dwindled and he was constantly mocking the fact that she was overweight, an ironic state of affairs given that a decade earlier, he had suffered at the hands of those who found his excess pounds a source of merriment.

The brothers had a sister who was later to recall how Steven – who she described as 'a bit backward' – was nervous whenever he was near his elder brother. She remembered how in 1995, the year of the attack on their grandmother, she saw the brothers together at a house in London.

She said: 'Steven was hiding. We saw him in the flat upstairs. He came to the window; he looked scared. Jason was behind him. A few days later, Steven had cigarette burns on his hands. He was petrified of Jason.'

In all probability, the presence of just one of the brothers in Peter's home could easily have spelled doom for him, but to have both under the same roof was to turn out to be a death sentence.

3

A CATALOGUE OF NEGLECT

I T IS impossible to catalogue the injuries that Peter Connelly received without wincing and it is perhaps even harder to look at the occasions when the child was either physically examined or his circumstances looked into by those in positions of authority and no positive action taken, action that might eventually have saved his life, without shaking one's head in disbelieve.

Peter Connelly's death shocked many people, but it was the sheer scale of the many chances to save his life and to protect him that were missed, and missed again, that practically bring tears to the eyes. It is necessary, therefore, to list them in some detail. Perhaps now is as good a time as any to detail the official involvement with little Peter before actually examining the torment that he had to live through.

In later chapters, we will examine in detail those who did – or didn't – do what, throughout their contact with Peter and what their subsequent reaction was. What went on in that hell of a home, in Penshurst Road, London N17, will be described in graphic detail.

To have a full understanding, not just of the treatment he received at the hands of his tormentors but also of the seemingly never-ending list of missed chances to help the child escape their clutches, it is necessary to 'leapfrog' in time through the sad narrative of his life, as only by doing that can the mistakes that led to his death be fully analysed.

When Connelly and the Barker brothers were eventually brought to trial at the Old Bailey in the winter of 2008, a damning dossier – with a timetable of official action (or inaction) – had already been compiled by lawyers for the prosecution. Additionally, in 2009 – also before Peter or his tormentors had been legally fully identified – the Haringey Local Safeguarding Children Board, under its new chairman Mr Graham Badman, released details of a serious case review that it had carried out into the scandal. Together, the two timetables give an official, comprehensive outline of the mistakes that were made as the opportunities to help slipped away, time and time again.

Graham Badman summed up what everyone who had read in horror about the case already knew: Peter's death 'could and should have been prevented.' He said that the social workers, lawyers, police and doctors who dealt with the case were 'lacking in urgency and lacking in thoroughness' and the review also found the agencies charged with protecting the child were not sceptical enough of the explanations given by his mother for his injuries and behaviour. The review concluded that Peter 'deserved better' from the people charged with protecting him.

Mr Badman told how the review found 'the actions of the

protecting professions involved with Baby P were lacking in urgency, lacking in thoroughness and insufficiently challenging to the child's mother'. The review also stated staff adopted a threshold of concern for taking children into care that was too high and the expectations of what could be achieved were too low. In its report, the review panel was also clear that every member of staff in every agency involved with Baby P was appropriately qualified, well motivated and wanted to do their best to safeguard him. However, the review concludes that his horrific death could – and should – have been prevented. It found that if doctors, lawyers, police and social workers had adopted a more urgent, thorough and challenging approach, the case would have been stopped in its tracks at the first serious incident. Baby P deserved better from the services which were set in place to protect him.'

Mr Badman added: 'I believe the most important lesson to be learned from this review is that professionals charged with ensuring child safety were not adequately sceptical of the explanations they were given for the apparent maltreatment of Baby P.'

The review was commissioned by Children's Secretary, Ed Balls after Baby P's death because of concerns over the conclusions of the first review.

Unlike the Haringey Review, the Old Bailey prosecution dossier named some of the professionals who dealt with Peter and those names subsequently appeared in newspapers and on television. Both the Badman Review and the prosecution dossier are reproduced here, albeit in truncated form, to give two official 'overviews' of the poor youngster's life.

Graham Badman's Review referred to many of the 'family members and significant others' purely by initials, but they can now be revealed as:

- Baby Peter (Peter Connelly)
- Ms A Baby P's mother (Tracey Connelly)
- Mr A Baby P's father (still not identifiable)
- Mrs AA Baby P's maternal grandmother (Mary O'Connor)
- Ms M Mother's friend and informal carer of Baby Peter (Angela Godfrey)
- Mr H Ms A's boyfriend (Steven Barker)
- Mr L (Jason Barker) and his 'girlfriend' F (still not identifiable) – resident at the time of death.

Also listed were the agencies involved with Peter during his brief life:

- Haringey's Children & Young People's Service (CYPS) (conducting enquiries and subsequently implementing agreed child protection plan)
- Haringey's Teaching Primary Care Trust (HtPCT) (providing health visiting, general practice, primary care mental health and school nursing services and supporting the child protection plan)
- Whittington Hospital NHS Trust (providing A&E, outpatient, day patient and in patient care and diagnostics, including pathology and radiology)
- North Middlesex University Hospital (NMUH) (providing A&E, ante- and post-natal care)

- Great Ormond Street Hospital (GOSH) providing on behalf of HtPCT paediatric medical services in Haringey, including the designated and named doctors for child protection and the paediatric A& E and inpatient services at NMUH
- Metropolitan Police Service (MPS) (working with, and alongside the CYPS to jointly investigate reported injuries to Peter)
- The Epic Trust and Family Welfare Association (FWA) (via the HARTS service, offering specific tenancy and family support using an Individual Support Plan)
- Two Haringey schools
- Haringey's Legal Services (providing legal advice to CYPS)
- Haringey's Strategic & Community Housing (organising provision of long-term temporary Housing Association accommodation for the family).

Below is the section of the lengthy Review by Haringey Local Safeguarding Children Board, which handled the dealings of those agencies in particular and the general 'officialdom' set in place from Peter's birth (described in the report as 'the first phase' of his life) to death:

Following Peter's birth at the North Middlesex University Hospital (NMUH) on 1st March 2006, a health visitor undertook a new birth visit. She found Peter to be developing well and breast feeding. Nevertheless, in the light of the family history, the case was placed in a 'blue folder', denoting a cause for concern.

Ms A brought and collected the older children from their school. Mr A was more involved in the early years of their attendance. During the summer of 2006 Mr H was seen with Ms A at the older children's school and introduced as a friend. On one occasion, Mr H came into school with two younger children in a buggy to collect one of the children, who was unwell.

On 18 September 2006 Ms A took Peter to the surgery with a cough and nappy rash. The GP recorded that in the course of the consultation she complained that the baby bruised easily, and that she might be accused of hurting him. Peter was six months old.

On 13 October 2006, Ms A again brought Peter to the surgery saying he had fallen down the stairs the previous day. The GP examined him and he had a bruise to the left breast and left cranium. He advised Ms A to install a stair-gate.

On 11 December 2006 Ms A telephoned the surgery and spoke to the GP. She said that Peter had a swelling on the head and asked what she should do. The GP invited her in so that he could examine the child. He told Ms A that he was going to refer Peter to the hospital.

At the Whittington Hospital a number of bruises were seen on his body and documented on a body map. Ms A said she did not know when or how the swelling on Peter's forehead had occurred. She attributed the other bruises to him climbing and falling and bruising easily, as well as slapping his body in play.

The body map made at the time shows extensive bruising to his buttocks and other bruises to his face and chest, including the swelling to his forehead which had triggered the referral from the GP. The test results indicated that he was not suffering with any condition which would mean that he would be susceptible to bruising easily.

While these enquiries continued, Peter remained in hospital.

The next day (12 December 2006) a strategy meeting was held. A contemporaneous note of the strategy discussion in social care records referred to 'pummelling' as a possible explanation for the significant bruising on his buttocks.

(The second phase of the investigation: from the strategy meeting on 12 December 2006 to the Initial Child Protection Conference on 22 December 2006)

The strategy meeting was attended by a social worker and a detective constable from the Metropolitan Police. There was clear concern about Peter's welfare and a decision was made that he could not return to the family home until the s.47 [Section 47, Child Protection] enquiries and police investigation had been completed. Mr A offered to take time off work to care for his son but this was not taken up because Ms A claimed he had slapped the children in the past. The notes of the meeting indicated the parents were separated and that the 'mother has a friend, Mr H. He is not alone with the children'.

On 13 December, the police officer and the social worker made a joint visit to the school to interview two of the older children. They were seen separately. Neither the school nor health services had concerns about their physical safety.

In a detailed letter dated 14 December the consultant paediatrician stated the combination of bruising seen 'is very suggestive of non-accidental injury'.

Peter was discharged from the hospital ward on 15 December to the care of Ms A's friend, Ms M.

During the visit to the hospital, the police officer interviewed Ms A under caution. Ms A provided the police officer with a number of hypothetical explanations for what may have caused the injuries to Peter. Ms A was unable to provide the police with any clear explanation for the injuries and denied she or her mother were responsible for them.

On 19 December the police arrested Ms A and Mrs AA. During their interview neither gave any specific explanations of how the injuries occurred, but gave the same possible causes as previously. They identified only Ms A and the children as living in the home, with Mrs AA staying occasionally. However there was no direct questioning of either about who else might access the home, or any associates. The police were aware that Mr A and Ms A were separated, and there was a man called Mr H, who was mentioned but only as a 'friend'.

(The third phase: the initial child protection conference) An initial child protection conference of those agencies involved was held on 22 December 2006.

The GP did not attend because he was not invited. Although the paediatrician from the Whittington Hospital was invited, she sent her apologies because she had an outpatient clinic and instead contributed a detailed written report. No one was sent instead to represent her views. A doctor from the Child Development Centre (CDC) was also invited, but gave apologies. The social worker presented a report that included information about Ms A's background history obtained from London Borough of Islington.

A legal representative of the local authority was present. Ms A also brought a legal representative. The police were represented by the investigating police officer. Their investigation into the injuries to Peter was continuing and they said that they understood that Peter would not be returned home until this was completed and noted that it was not recorded in the minutes.

Ms A was not able to give any explanation of how Peter's injuries had occurred.

Peter had a good relationship with his father, which was seen when he went for his bone scan, when only his father could calm his distress.

In summarising, the Chair reminded the conference that the paediatrician at the Whittington Hospital was of the opinion that the injuries to Peter were non-accidental in nature. No adult had given any explanation of how Peter sustained those injuries and who was with him at the time. This was of great concern for a 9-month-old baby. Eventually Peter was registered for both physical abuse and neglect.

Most participants agreed that one of the other children should also be registered for neglect. None of the conference members supported the registration of other children in the family.

(The fourth phase: from 23 December 2006 to the first review child protection conference on 16 March 2007)

During the period following the initial child protection conference, Peter and another child were seen regularly by the social worker, and collectively very frequently by the health visitor, the FWA project worker and the GP. The older children were seen almost daily during the week as they attended school regularly. What was seen of the relationship between the mother and the younger children was assessed positively.

Ms M, with whom Peter was staying, reported he had bruises on his testes and claimed they had been caused by hospital staff doing a scan. The bruising on his buttocks had gone.

Social workers visited the family home on 24, 27 and 29 December 2006. Ms A saw her son three times on Christmas Day.

The legal view, given orally immediately following the child protection conference and confirmed by email, on 29 December 2006, was that the threshold for care proceedings had been met, but this did not prompt the Children & Young People's Service to initiate care proceedings in respect of Peter.

The first core group meeting was held on 10 January 2007 and Ms A attended with Peter. A review strategy meeting was held on 24 January and agreed that if the injuries were non-accidental, it was not clear who the perpetrator was. The police agreed that Peter could go home once Ms A made alternative arrangements for the dogs.

Peter returned home on 26 January 2007. The family moved to their new home on 19 February 2007. There was a change of social worker.

Over the next month all the children were seen by another GP in the practice – they were judged to be happy and well. There was a social worker's visit on 20 February and all the children were seen; the social worker observed a good relationship between Peter and his mother.

On 5 March, the school nurse phoned the social worker to

say that she had observed Ms A that day shouting loudly and slapping the cheek of one of Peter's siblings outside the school. The sibling was seen alone and confirmed the assault. Ms A had already agreed to attend a parenting programme and the social worker proposed no further action.

On visits to the home on 5 March and on 8 March the social worker saw Peter, happy and smiling.

On 13 March the social worker interviewed Mr A. This was the first time that he had been seen since the December admission to the Whittington Hospital. Mr A wanted more contact with his children and he was advised by the social worker to get legal advice. He said that Ms A had a boyfriend whom he had seen at the family home. Later, Ms A angrily denied this to the social worker. Mr A said that he did not believe that Ms A would hit the children.

At the review child protection conference on 16 March the social worker was to increase the frequency of her announced and unannounced visits to weekly. The plan now was for monthly contact with the health visitor, either at the home or at the clinic.

(The fifth phase: from the first review child protection conference to 18 July 2007)

On a visit to the PCMHW (Primary Care Mental Health Worker) on 23 March, Ms A was angry and upset with the social work service because she said that the high frequency of visits she was receiving were preventing her from relaxing and enjoying her children.

A core group meeting was held on 29 March 2007.

At 4.40 pm on 9 April, Ms A took Peter to A & E at the North Middlesex Hospital. The triage nurse noted a large boggy swelling to the left side of his head. Mother's account was that four days earlier he had been pushed against a marble fireplace by another child of his age. Apart from being grizzly over the next two days, he had seemed fine but he had woken that morning with neck pain, holding his head to the left side. He had a small round bruise on his right cheek, a rash on the back of his arms and obvious head lice. Tests were done for meningitis because of the rash and neck stiffness, although this was eventually ruled out. Body maps indicated bruises and scratches on his face, head and body.

Ms A said that she had a friend in the waiting room who witnessed the fall and she was fearful Peter would be taken into care because he was on the Child Protection Register. (The friend is now thought to have been Mr H.) Peter was admitted to a ward for 48 hours' observation. On two evenings a man referred to as his father was present, but didn't stay. Ms A was reported to have remained with him throughout his stay. It is not certain who was caring for the other children during this time.

A hospital nurse confirmed to the social worker that the child had been brought in because he was injured, but this was not viewed as non-accidental because the mother stated that the injury was caused by another child. It is reasonable to infer that staff had been misdirected as to the possible cause and they speculated that he had experienced some kind of allergic reaction. By this time there was no sign of the original injury. The social work team agreed the discharge. No referral was made to the police.

Peter was discharged on 11 April 2007. The discharge report of 17 April from the hospital referred to Ms A reporting a trivial head injury caused by playing with siblings a few days before admission.

The social worker next visited the home on 24 April and saw Peter and the other children. Peter appeared unsteady on his feet and the social worker discussed this with Ms A. A core group meeting was held on 2 May.

On 9 May, the health visitor saw Peter at home and he was observed as a lively and active toddler. He was clean and appropriately dressed. On 16 May, the FWA project worker made a home visit and saw Peter and one of the other children playing happily. Then, on 21 May, all the children were seen by the social worker and were well and playing happily.

On 1 June, the social worker made an unannounced visit to the home and observed a bruise under Peter's chin. Ms A said it was caused by a squabble with the child of a friend. The social worker requested that Ms A take Peter to the GP. Peter was taken to A&E at the NMUH, who were aware that he was on the Child Protection Register.

At the hospital, a history was taken. Ms A's account was that a friend had been staying between 25 and 28th May, and she thought the bruises were caused by rough play with the friend's 22-month-old toddler. During the consultation he banged his head once and fell twice onto his bottom. There were multiple bruises and scratches of different ages on his body and only some could be put down to normal rough play and falls. On his lower right leg was a grab mark bruise that doctors were particularly concerned about; Ms A said that she had grabbed Peter by his leg to prevent him falling off a sofa. The social worker was happy for the child to be discharged home because a friend would be staying with the family over the weekend. The social worker said she would pick things up on the following Monday.

The police were informed and elected not to undertake a joint investigation, but to allow the social worker to look into it and to call them in, if she felt they had a role.

On 3 June, when the health visitor contacted the hospital, they added that Peter also had an infected finger when seen, that the findings were inconclusive and that Ms A was observed to have bonded well with the child.

The police were convinced the injuries were non-accidental and requested a strategy meeting be arranged. This took place on 4 June 2007. Agreement was reached to: undertake s.47 enquiries, hold an urgent legal planning meeting to consider care proceedings, fast-track a paediatric assessment, make arrangements for Peter to be supervised at the family home by the family friend Ms M, agree a contract with Ms A and find a childminder to assist with childcare during the day. A joint investigation by the police and children's social care was ongoing. Ms A was interviewed by the police and she offered a variety of possible causes for the injuries and no admissions were made.

Ms A and Ms M (the family friend) met the team manager to sign a written agreement to the effect that Ms A and Peter would not be left alone together. There would also be a childminder for Peter and one of the other children on particular days. This agreement was to be reviewed in two weeks.

The police felt that while their investigation into the injuries was still taking place Peter should be removed from his mother's care.

On 8 June 2007, the review child protection conference was held. The social worker took the conference through the injuries of 1 June and said they could not all be explained by Ms A's account; the reasonable conclusion from the medical examination was that the injuries were probably non-accidental. Following this, the meeting was informed that a legal planning meeting was to be held within the next week to inform future decision-making. The conference Chair expressed her concern that Peter was experiencing the same injuries for which he was originally placed on a Child Protection Plan. In addition, if they were caused by Peter's own behaviour, as his mother claimed, then they should occur continuously rather than in a pattern of serious, but intermittent injury.

On 15 June the FWA project worker made a home visit. Ms A's friend, Mr H, was present. Ms A was upset at being arrested for the injuries to Peter. She was happy to speak in front of Mr H because he knew everything.

On 19 June, Baby Peter and one of the other children were seen by the social worker at the childminder's. Both interacted well with the three other children being looked after. The childminder did not convey any concerns. A core group meeting was also held on 20 June.

On 29 June, the social worker had a message from the childminder that Ms A had taken Peter away. The social worker tried to contact Ms A on three occasions that day without success. On 2 July, the social worker made contact with Ms A, who said that she was looking after her uncle in Cricklewood. She would be returning on either 4 or 9 July, depending on his health.

The school electronic attendance printout shows that two of the older children were away from school between 29 June and 5 July.

On 9 July, the social worker made contact with Ms A, who was back in Haringey. She was at a Walk In Clinic (WIC) for Peter. At a home visit that day, the social worker saw all the children. Peter's ear was red and looked sore. Ms A showed the social worker the medication prescribed at the WIC.

(The sixth phase: from 18 July to 3 August – the final two weeks of events leading to Peter's death)

On 18 July Ms A and Peter were seen by the clinic's health visitor – Peter's weight had reduced to the 25th centile (percentage point) although his appetite was described as good. It was reported by Ms A that he had been seen at the Walk In Clinic on 16 July (although this was, in fact, on 9 July) and treated with cream for his head scabs. It was noted that Peter was on a Child Protection Plan and was well groomed and nourished, and that there were no unexplained physical injuries. He had also been given antibiotics for his ear infection. His left ear was red on the outside and his lobe appeared to be infected. Ms A explained that she had caused the bruising around his ear while trying to clean it. Ms A was advised again to go to the WIC at the NMUH. The health visitor contacted the social worker, who tried without success to contact Ms A to discuss her concerns.

On 19 July, Ms A took Peter to the WIC at NMUH, where they were subsequently referred to A&E. A history was taken and he was assessed and described as alert and looking around. Peter had an infected scalp with bloody scabs, head lice and blood around the left ear, where he had been scratching. He looked grubby and the middle finger of his right hand was infected in the nail bed. Ms A said that he had developed a hives reaction on his head to red Leicester cheese, which became infected from scratching. The infection was not investigated by doctors. A&E phoned the emergency duty team.

On 23 July, the childminder phoned the social worker to say that she could no longer care for Peter and the other child because of his scalp infection and their head lice. The social worker phoned Ms A and expressed concern that the infection was taking so long to clear up and said that Ms A should take him to see the GP. On 26 July, the social worker phoned Ms A after she had taken Peter to see the GP. According to Ms A, the GP was unable to prescribe more antibiotics, was not concerned and thought that Peter might have had an allergic reaction to the head lice treatment. The GP recognised the need for concern, but did nothing because he thought others would do something, and the child was being seen at the Child Development Centre in a few days.

On 25 July, the legal planning meeting took place and the decision was made that the case did not, at present, meet the threshold for care proceedings but that the position should be reviewed in light of further reports expected.

On 30 July, all the children were seen on a planned home

visit by the social worker on their own and with Ms A. Peter was in the buggy, alert and smiling, but overtired. His ear was sore and slightly inflamed. On the top of his head was white cream and Ms A thought the infection had improved. Peter's face was smeared with chocolate and the social worker asked that it be cleaned off. The family friend took him away to do so and he did not reappear before the social worker left. Ms A said she had a GP appointment and mentioned grab marks on Peter. She was worried about being accused of harming him.

On 31 July, the police met with the Crown Prosecution Service (CPS), who advised no further action on both of the investigations.

On 1 August, Ms A took Peter to the CDC appointment, accompanied by her friend, Ms M, whom the doctor took to be a foster carer for Peter. The referral had made clear that Peter was on the Child Protection Register, but not that he was the focus of current enquiries for injuries. Peter was unwell, with a temperature and a runny nose; he had visible bruises. Ms A shared her concerns about his behaviour. A paediatric social, developmental and family history was taken. Ms A became tearful when reporting that CYPS had accused her of causing the bruises to Peter. She said that he was a much-wanted boy. His weight was now on the 9th centile – a considerable loss.

The doctor concluded he was unwell and miserable due to a possible viral infection. He had a history of recurrent bruising and recurrent infections; a history of abnormal behaviours – aggression, head-butting, head banging and hyperactivity – and there was a possibility that he might have some underlying metabolic disorder. In her notes of 8 August, the doctor stated that she had advised Ms A to go to the GP or the hospital A&E, if Peter did not get better. He was not examined by the GP. No reports had been provided of his previous admissions and attendances at the Whittington and NMUH for possible non-accidental injuries, nor were they sought.

On 2 August, Ms A was seen by the police at the Social Services offices and told neither prosecutions would be pursued.

On 3 August, the London Ambulance Service responded to a 999 call at 11.35am. The caller was Ms A, who reported a 17-month-old child, on antibiotics, who was now not moving. She reported to the crew that she had last seen him at approximately 1am and that he had recently been unwell with a fungal infection. Ms A travelled in the ambulance to NMUH with Peter. He was pronounced dead at 12.19pm.

Mention has already been made earlier of the prosecution dossier prepared for the Old Bailey trial. It was this series of blunders, in addition to the actual injuries Peter received, that was to horrify the nation. The dossier should be read closely in conjunction with the Review prepared by Graham Badman's team. Of course, there are areas of repetition and occasionally some slight differences in dates, but it too highlights what went wrong with Peter Connelly's care. Perhaps what it also does is to lay bare to an even greater extent, if that is possible, the frightening scale of the failure of care the child suffered even in the midst of constant contact between the family and Social Services, various medical staff and police.

The dossier, shown to the jury during the Old Bailey trial and subsequently made public, documented 78 separate occasions when Baby P was seen by Haringey's social workers, health visitors and doctors.

Like the previous report, it starts with Peter's birth and details the first routine contacts he had with doctors and health clinics but then it goes on to say that by May 2006, his mother had begun to complain that he was vomiting after his feeds. Later, she told doctors that he also seemed to bruise easily – her explanation for his constant injuries.

But by October/November 2006 – when Steven Barker had moved in and she had begun a new relationship with her sadistic lover – the entries become more worrying and by the middle of the month read: 'Doctor. Bruising to head & chest/accidental fall downstairs'.

It is the first of many occasions when Peter suffered an injury but his evil mother had an explanation that was all too easily accepted.

A fortnight before that first Christmas he was admitted to hospital with a 2-inch blood clot across his forehead and bruises to his chest and shoulder. Connelly said they must have happened while his grandmother was looking after him.

However, doctors – including consultant paediatrician Heather McKinnon – agreed they were 'very suggestive of non-accidental injury' and called in Social Services and the police's Child Abuse investigation team. The next day, social workers held a strategy meeting and a foster family was arranged for him, but the plan was not followed through and he was placed with a family friend, Angela Godfrey.

On 19 December, Peter's mother and grandmother were

arrested on suspicion of assaulting him and three days later, he was put on Haringey's Child Protection Register over fears that he was the victim of physical abuse and neglect. Meanwhile, he seemed thrive, uninjured, while in Miss Godfrey's care and even put on some weight.

On 26 January, his mother was seen by a mental health worker and Peter returned to her after Haringey said that she would be given parenting classes and supported by social workers. The family's allocated social worker Maria Ward noticed a red mark on his face on 22 March, on her fifth visit to the house. His mother said he fell on a table. Miss Ward did not consider the injury to be 'significant'.

On 9 April, he appears to have suffered another 'fall', when his mother took him to their GP with bruising and swelling to the head. She told the doctor that another child pushed him into a marble fireplace, causing the bruising. A social worker visit later that month stated 'no concerns' even though Peter had been referred to a Child Development Clinic over concerns that he was banging his own head against the floor and walls of the family home.

On 1 June, Miss Ward made an unannounced visit to the family home and saw that Peter's face was red and bruised; at her request he was taken to hospital for a Child Protection Order check and doctors found 12 separate areas of bruising and a 'grip mark' on his leg. Police re-arrested his mother over fears that she was assaulting him yet two months later his mother told the GP that she was 'feeling stressed by Social Services & accusations of harming baby,' the dossier notes.

Then, with Peter's short time on Earth already running out,

came one of the most sickening of all the incidents when Connelly and Barker cunningly smeared his face and hands with chocolate and nappy cream to disguise his injuries from social workers.

Just two days later, he was taken to the Child Development Clinic at St Ann's Hospital Tottenham and examined by locum paediatrician Sabah Al Mayyat, who failed to spot that he had 8 broken ribs and his spine had been snapped.

The dossier notes only that he was 'quite miserable and crying' and that it was 'not possible to make full examination'. Two days later, Peter Connelly was pronounced dead.

Below is the full prosecution timetable of Peter's life and death:

1st March 2006: Baby P born

22nd March: First home visit by health visitor Yvonne Douglas. P has oral thrush

24th March: Family GP Jerome Ikwueke sees P for oral thrush

7th April: Weighed at baby clinic by Yvonne Douglas

13th April: Six-week examination by Dr Ikwueke

2nd May: GP visit for diarrhoea and vomiting

4th May: Mother attends health clinic with P, seen by Yvonne Douglas

22nd May: First vaccinations for meningitis and diphtheria, pertussis [whooping cough] and tetanus at GP clinic

28th May: P vomiting after feeds, mother calls out-of-hours emergency service

4th June: GP visit for pain, diarrhoea and vomiting

9th June: P's mother seen for depression by mental health worker Karolina Jamry

19th June: GP visit, second immunisations

11th August: P's mother seen re: problems in her marriage by Ms Jamry

15th September: Home visit by health visitor Yvonne Douglas

19th September: Seen by GP for nappy rash

13th October: Seen by GP for bruising to head and chest, mother claims accidental fall down stairs

17th November: GP visit for upper respiratory tract infection and thrush

11th December: Admitted to Whittington Hospital. Bruising to forehead and nose, sternum and right shoulder/breast

12th December: P examined and referred to Child Abuse investigation team, seen by DC Angela Slade

13th December: P examined on ward by consultant paediatrician Heather Mackinnon

14th December: P examined on ward by Dr Mackinnon

15th December: P discharged into care of Angela Godfrey. Police investigation begins

18th December: Social worker Agnes White visits mother at home

19th December: P's mother and grandmother arrested and interviewed at Hornsey Police Station in North London

21st December: P's leg X-rayed at hospital

22nd December: Mother attends child protection conference with Haringey social workers and Dr Mackinnon

24 December: Emergency Duty Team visits Angela Godfrey's home to check on P

27th December: Social worker Agnes White visits P at Godfrey home. Returns later unannounced

29th December: Agnes White returns for check on P's contact with mother

9th January 2007: Angela Godfrey takes P to health clinic for thrush on buttocks, seen by Yvonne Douglas

12th January: P's leg X-rayed again at hospital

16th January: Agnes White second check on P's contact with mother

17th January: P's leg X-rayed again at hospital

19th January: Mother seen by Ms Jamry

25th January: GP visit for nappy rash

26th January: Repeat visit by Agnes White to check on P's contact with mother. On same day, mother seen by Ms Jamry

2nd February: P's third set of vaccinations and Maria Ward allocated as social worker

8th February: Preliminary assessment of mother by unspecified official Caroline Sussex

18th February: P and mother moved to new address in Haringey

22nd February: Social worker Maria Ward's first home visit

27th February: Miss Ward attends case conference at Haringey

2nd March: Miss Ward and health visitor Paulette Thomas visit mother at home

5th March: Miss Ward questions mother after school nurse sees her slap a child

6th March: Unannounced visit by Miss Ward

8th March: Visit by Miss Ward

14th March: Visit by Family Support Service worker Marie Lockhart

16th March: Haringey Child Protection conference with mother, attended by Miss Ward and Miss Lockhart

20th March: Mother and P videoed at parenting class

22nd March: Miss Ward visit

23rd March: One year check at health clinic

29th March: Haringey case conference

9th April: P seen by GP with bruising to face. Mother claims pushed into fireplace by another child

9th April: P admitted North Middlesex hospital for bruising and swelling to head

10th April: P referred to child development clinic by social worker who sees him 'headbanging'

11th April: Discharged from North Middlesex

12th April: Child Protection meeting at North Middlesex

24th April: Miss Ward home visit

3rd May: Mother and P attend parenting class

9th May: Planned home visit by Health Visitor Ms Thomas

16th May: Family support visit by Ms Lockhart

18th May: GP visit for hives (allergic reaction)

21st May: Miss Ward visit

1st June: Miss Ward unannounced visit, reports mother to police over bruises to P. P taken to North Middlesex for check-up

5th June: Mother interviewed under caution at Hornsey Police Station

6th June: P seen by Ms Thomas at health clinic

7th June: More immunisations at GP surgery and child protection meeting at North Middlesex

8th June: Police take photos of P and seize toy from home

12th June: Registered childminder Anne Walker takes P for day care for ten days

15th June: Ms Lockhart visits home

19th June: Miss Ward visits childminder

20th June: Case conference at Haringey

21st June: P and mother attend parenting class

5th July: Mother and P attend parenting class

9th July: Mother takes P to North Middlesex with ear infection

11th July: Miss Ward visit

18th July: P seen at health clinic for scalp and ear infection

19th July: Mother and P attend parenting class and attend North Middlesex with previous infection

26th July: GP visit for head lice and blood in ear

30th July: Case conference at Haringey, Miss Ward home visit, mother feeling stressed

1st August: P seen at St Ann's Hospital by locum paediatrician Sabah Al-Zayyat

2nd August: Mother told police to take no further action over assault allegations

3rd August: 11:36am, 999 call. 11.40 Ambulance arrives. 11.43 Ambulance leaves.

11.49 Ambulance arrives hospital

12.10pm P pronounced dead. Police called. 13.30 body maps completed. 13.45 Mother arrested.

Two lists, one conclusion: Peter Connelly lived an appalling life and died a horrifying death.

So what exactly did go on behind that shabby door in north London? What was Peter forced to endure in the months leading up to his untimely death?

4

HOUSE OF HORROR

THE LIFE that Peter Connelly led in that run-down house in Tottenham almost defies belief. From the outside it looked like any other shabby, unloved semi-detached home. Certainly not colour supplement material, but nothing exceptional given the weary, grubby area it was in. It was the hidden horror inside that was so disturbing.

Knowing the litany of errors in the handling of the case by virtually everyone involved, as detailed in the previous chapter, now is an appropriate time to investigate exactly what happened to Peter within the four walls of that house.

It is impossible to give exact times and dates for the abuse he received and therefore link those attacks chronologically with the numerous meetings with social workers and medical staff. The only way to do so would be if Connelly and the Barker brothers had kept diary of dates for their savagery. Of course, that was hardly likely to happen, they weren't the kind to keep diaries.

Later, it emerged that a total of 19 doctors and health workers saw Peter on 33 occasions in the 8 months before his death. Although some were concerned about his wellbeing, it is obvious that for a large part of that time, the torment and abuse he suffered to a savage extent remained undetected. So just what did happen there?

Steven Barker's cruelty knew no end. He took delight in cutting off Peter's fingertips with a Stanley knife and pulling his nails out with pliers, as well as smacking the boy on his private parts with a shoe. Once, he smashed the boy's head into the fireplace, only for Connelly to lie and say her son had been pushed there by another child. Barker would also bite Peter in an attempt to 'train' his pet Rottweiler Kaizer and other dogs in the house to attack him and once, he rammed a bottle into his mouth so hard that he cut the boy's lips.

On other occasions, Barker – who had an interest in Satanism, as well as Nazis – deliberately dropped Peter some six feet onto the floor and he would grab him by the throat and hurl him into his cot. He also pressed down so hard on the child's windpipe that he turned blue.

One of the others living in the house, Jason's teenage girlfriend, witnessed many of the attacks, including perhaps the most horrendous of all, which left Peter paralysed from the waist down.

The girl, who was 15 at the time and cannot be identified, told after the boy's death how Barker had Peter on his knee one afternoon while he was watching the Jeremy Kyle show on television. He liked to watch TV, lying on the sofa, smoking dope and swilling can after can of lager: 'He sat smirking on the sofa, smoking cannabis and playing with Peter like he was a rag doll. Then I suddenly heard a loud crack that echoed through the house as the baby's little backbone snapped in half. He let out a gut-wrenching scream. It was so loud, I got up and went into the garden and put my hands over my ears to block it out.'

When a post-mortem examination was carried out, it revealed that one of Peter's teeth had been knocked out and swallowed, a finger and toenail had been torn off, he was infested with lice and had bruises and cuts to his face and ears.

The 15-year-old also told how Peter's fate was finally sealed because he had been crying at night, no doubt in terrible pain: 'He was wailing and wailing in his cot. He just wouldn't stop, but he'd been lying in his urine and faeces for days. Then the step-dad came down and said, "I'll sort it." He went into the room, slammed the door shut and suddenly the crying stopped.'

It was a vicious blow given by Barker that forced the teeth out and into Peter's stomach.

The girl continued: 'I discovered him dead in the cot at around 9am. He'd gone a funny colour, a pale blue, and was stiff. I told his mum he wasn't breathing, but she waited until 11.30am before dialling 999 for an ambulance.'

By then Barker and his elder brother Jason, a member of the National Front, had left the house with Peter's blood-stained, smelly bedclothes, which they tried to dump in a cemetery to hide any evidence of his ordeal.

The girl recalled: 'It was disgusting and perverted, what went on in that house. It went way beyond cruel, it was sadistic. Steve would shake Peter, punch him, swing him around by his legs and spin him round on the computer chair until he came flying off and hit his head on the floor. Then he'd pick him up and do it again. He put his thumb down over the poor mite's windpipe until he turned blue and stopped breathing. Then he just laughed, let go and pushed it in again even harder to see how much he could take.

'He'd pinch the baby's little fingernails and squeeze them until he screamed. And he lanced off the tops of the tot's fingers with a Stanley knife, like you would a boil. He said it made it easier for him to then use the pliers to grip onto the fingernails and rip them off. It makes me shudder.

'He made Peter kneel in front of him, with blood oozing from the ends of his fingers, and hold out his hands for more punishment. Not content with that, he'd hold him above his head and then just drop him on the floor.'

At one stage there were at least eight people living in the house: Peter, his mother and her other children, the Barker brothers and the teenager. There were also three dogs, Steven Barker's Rottweiler, an Alsatian and a Staffordshire bull terrier.

The girl remembers that Steven Barker would lay Peter on his back in the middle of the room and bite him and growl in front of the dogs. He bit into his head, his arms, his body and his legs. Then he'd get the dogs to copy this disgusting act. He felt it was all part of a 'toughening up' process. As well as this cruelty, he would use a shoe to hit the baby on his genitals and often wrapped him tightly in blankets, leaving him for hours in his cot to dehydrate.

Not surprisingly, there were never any bedtime stories for Peter. He would be literally thrown into the cot. The teenager recalled: 'He was picked up off the floor like a rag doll and tossed into his cot. At night I'd hear him crying and head-butting the wooden bars on his cot. It went on for hours.'

After his spine had been snapped and just a few days before his death, Peter was taken for a walk in the woods by Barker and kept falling down, unable even to stand. The teenage girl was with them at the time and even she feared the child was badly injured and his back might be broken. He was never to walk properly again.

The girl also witnessed the last full day of Peter's life, 2 August – the same day that Tracey Connelly was informed that she would not face prosecution over Peter – it was a day when poor Peter, undoubtedly in constant pain, suffered yet again.

At 11pm, Steven Barker told her to watch as he squeezed the boy's fingers really hard. It must have been excruciatingly painful, yet Peter didn't scream. No doubt he no longer had the energy or the willpower to do so. He didn't even have the strength to sit up and kept falling over. The child looked desperately ill and was sweating profusely. Steven Barker's response to that was to hit him on the head and even though this was a cruel blow, it forced no reaction from the child, who was by now in a terrible condition, unable even to respond to any more pain.

Even Barker's heartless brother Jason said it looked as though the child was dying, only for his kid brother to say that he thought he was 'fine'.

'Fine' – how could anyone be 'fine' with over 50 injuries to their body, following a brief life in which some days 23 hours were spent in a cot, locked in a small, dark room with the curtains drawn? For hours he would go unchecked and unchanged – Steven Barker liked to be in charge. He was a control freak and therefore didn't like anyone else going into the room or even changing the baby's nappy.

Illiterate Barker found one way of amusing himself that didn't involve lager, vodka or beer – he would force Peter to follow commands, like a dog. At the click of a finger, he would have to sit with his head bent between his legs. Then, some 20 minutes later, a second click would be the signal that he could sit upright again.

So what was Tracey Connelly doing while her only son was undergoing such torment? Most mornings she would lie in bed and when she eventually did get up, she would watch porn on the Internet or spend her state-provided money on online poker betting. Peter's cries went unheeded, his battered body relentlessly being destroyed.

But Tracey was too busy on her computer to tend to him anyway, even if she had decided to. Yet, without a hint of shame, she even boasted online that one of her favourite things was 'being a mum.'

The teenage girl said: 'She ignored all the kids and let them do what they wanted. She was scared of her partner, though – we all were. Day after day, I heard screaming coming from Baby P's cot, but I didn't dare go in there. His nappy went unchanged for so long his skin just rotted away. His bottom was red raw, blistered and covered in sores.'

Yet this scenario was allowed to continue despite visits from care workers. Tracey Connelly, with her childhood background of lying to those in authority, or at the very least concealing the truth from them with evasions and mock ignorance, carried this off with aplomb. Peter eventually outgrew milk and jars of baby food, so he had to scrounge broken bits of biscuit from the floor. All the time, the teenager said, Connelly simply lied to social and health care workers, as she did to family and friends, keeping Barker's cruelty from the world.

'She explained away pus-filled, infected cuts all over the baby's face with a string of rubbish that was simply accepted by professionals paid to look after him. She's a despicable mother, total scum. She told them he was clumsy and kept falling over and bumping his head. It was all lies.'

Incredibly, one health visitor watched on a visit when Peter sat in the back garden, shovelling fistfuls of dirt into his mouth.

There was a large bruise to his forehead and he seemed quiet and withdrawn. Instead of setting alarm bells ringing, the injury was explained away – like countless other blows to the child – with a barely plausible story about him falling from his toy car.

'I couldn't believe these social workers kept falling for it,' said the girl.

A few days before he died, and with his face covered in bruises and cuts, Peter received a final visit from social worker Maria Ward. This was to become the notorious occasion when chocolate was used to hide his injuries. The 'miss' on the social worker's part has been well documented, but the teenage girl gives a fascinating account of what happened: 'Peter was in such a state his mum was worried. She actually said the social worker would have to be an idiot not to notice there was something wrong, so she melted chocolate in a saucepan and smeared it over his face to cover the injuries. Then she laid him in his buggy because he was too limp for the high chair and put a chocolate biscuit in his hand. He had head lice anyway, so she put cream on to cover up his bleeding cuts. The social worker didn't spot a thing. The mum couldn't believe her luck when she just had a quick look at Peter in his buggy and said, "Hello, little fella!" That was it. He was pushed into the kitchen. Door shut. That was the last time he was seen alive by anyone outside the house.'

If that description isn't tearinducing in itself, the girl added in a newspaper interview that she gave: 'The heartbreaking thing is he smiled at the woman. Sitting in that buggy with his back broken, eight broken ribs, fingernails missing, toenail missing and a nappy full of excrement and he still managed a smile. If she had just taken a second to look properly, to pick him up and look at him, she'd have realised there was something gravely wrong. All the social worker said before she left the house was, "If you're taking him out later, make sure you wash his face." It's a disgrace.'

When she gave evidence at the subsequent trial, Maria Ward said that she visited the house days before Peter's death for a prearranged meeting. She found the boy in his pushchair, his bruises covered up with chocolate. 'He had eaten a chocolate biscuit and there was chocolate over his face,' she told the court. 'He had chocolate on his hands and face.' She said that she asked the mother to wipe his face before they went out and the mother started cleaning him. Miss Ward noted that the boy had an infected scalp, which was covered in white cream, and an ear infection. But she added: 'He appeared well. He smiled when I spoke to him.' The case worker said that she had been content to leave the boy with his mother because she appeared to be co-operative and properly supported.

Whatever appearance she may have presented to some, Tracey Connelly seemed to care more for her two dogs, an Alasatian called Lady and Lucky, the 'Staffie', than she did for her own children. She could hardly have been accused of being too busy looking after her house either, as in a staggering understatement she said in one computer message: 'I hate housework.'

This wasn't the only message she sent via the Internet, to which she was practically addicted. As Peter suffered unimaginable abuse at the hands of her boyfriend, Connelly went online to boast about her sex life, heavy drinking and to complain that she was bored. Soon after moving to Penshurst Road, she wrote: 'My life is crazy. Have moved house and I'm loving my new place. Just need to try and move one more time tho, as want out of London.'

One day, when she took Peter to a hospital for an ear infection, she went online afterwards to demand that someone send her some jokes to cheer her up.

Many social networking sites are a source of inane, vacuous comments, but even by that standard Connelly's illiterate ramblings sunk to a sad depth.

In another one missive she says: 'well im just chillin after another busy day in the life of Tracey ..my house is a crazy place. im going to bed soon just having a cig and watching poker on telly. wish i was in the pub playing pool tho lol [laugh out loud] never mind love you all lol

'why do i do it again and again i went out thursday to the pub and was drinking cocktails dont ask why and large vodkas and cokes i got really drunk like a t*** then this morning i had to get up... ouch my head hurt was all i could think about and it hurt all bloody day every sound however small was like a bomb in my head

'how do you no when your in love could someone please tell me lol... love is a stupid thing.

'hello everyone hope everyone is ok im very tired have spent the week being a dirty girl not saying how lol. just getting a night off so thought i would chill online.'

Months later, the mother was back on her blog. By now, police and Social Services had been alerted over fears that Peter was being abused and his mother had been arrested twice on suspicion of assaulting him, but is more interested in her birthday plans:

'its my birthday tomorrow im going to be 26 i cant wait going pub to play some pool then having a few drinks at my house wanted to go clubbing but cant be bothered. we going to drive the whole street crazy will update you on sat how it went... love crazy xxxxxxxxxxxxxxxxxxxxxxx'

'well its the morning after my birthday and im f***** feel like death had a great night with lots of friends round'

'im really bored can you lot send me some jokes or something to make me laugh. need to find something to laugh about cause if i dont i think im going to go crazy. please please PLEASE HELP!!!!!!!!!!!!!!!!'

'ok people you know how this works i write a line then you guys write in the coments the next line. see if we can make a funny story ok x'

'ok so why is it when i want to chat i just get bugged with people wanting cyber sex?'

Less than two weeks before Peter died, Connelly complained

on her blog that she was been the target of 'desperate ferrets' who wanted to have online sex chats with her and on a day that Peter had been to a health clinic for his infected head wounds and bruises, all his mother appeared to care about was starting a chain letter.

In one email she wrote: 'Life is bullshit ... People should stay away from me as I have always messed up everyone who's close to me. I'm a jinx to all I know' and she posted on her Bebo website: 'My fella is nuts but being in love is great.'

Connelly even had the nerve, on her site, to describe her job as 'professional mum' while boasting of sex with her brutal partner and regular binge-drinking.

Astonishingly, she was to add her 'baby boy' was the 'coolest' person she had met and says the best thing to happen to her was 'becoming a mum'. She was nearer the mark when she added that her hobbies were 'drinking, football and having a damn good time'. Stating, 'When I drink, I drink' and named her three favourite brands of beer – all strong lagers.

In November 2006, she wrote: 'It's funny when you meet someone and fall in love. You spend as much time as poss kissing and touching and having sex. You want to make them feel so good you just can't get enough of each other. It's great.'

In her profile she described herself as a 'crazy mum', although she hardly mentions her children at all. But she is not so reluctant to talk about her lifestyle, saying she only goes to bed: 'when I feel like it'.

In another post – presumably referring to Steven Barker – she said: 'Sorry I not been about people. I have spent the last week being a dirty bitch' as well as revealing that she was naked as she sat at her computer.

Connelly listed her favourite cocktail as Tequila Sunrise and her choice in films was either Kung-Fu or any other martial arts.

Bizarrely she even depicted herself as a Good Samaritan in one message, saying she dialled 999 because a neighbour had left their car lights on, only for them complain: 'They said they would be there ASAP. I waited 1 hour and 20 mins in the freezing cold for them to come. I called them back and they said they might be another hour as they was busy. Fine. Is it time to stop helping others?'

If many people had ignored or failed to see the plight of Peter Connelly, one who did not was Ann Walker, the childminder who cared for him in the final few weeks of his life in order to 'give his mum a break.'

When the scandal broke out, she revealed: 'He was dying. I told them about his state. I said things were not right, but nothing was done. If someone had taken action we would not be mourning the loss of a baby's life. The warning signs were all there.'

Walker was ordered to report any injuries she found to social workers and said: 'It was upsetting. Four or five times I phoned about bruises, marks, nappy rash and dried blood in his ear. He always smelt of vomit, his clothes were dirty. His fingers were black and nails were broken. Once he pulled off one of his fingernails. He had a large scab on his head that would weep blood. When I took him out of the highchair, I had to wash the blood off it. He was in a terrible state.

'I asked how all this happened. Maria Ward said, "We've been told he's accident prone."'

The 999 call (from Penshurst Road on the morning of 3 August 2007) came late, months too late, to save poor Peter. Yet even after his death Tracey Connelly seemed remote from the tragedy. The Barker brothers had fled the house and Connelly was out on bail when she met a neighbour: 'I thought it was unusual to see her because she'd not lived here for a while,' the neighbour remembered.

'I asked her how things were and she told me that her little boy had died of cot death. I put my arm round her and consoled her, but there seemed to be little emotion. A couple of days later, I bumped into her outside and she broke off the conversation to rush upstairs and take care of her pet Alsatian. That same day she called down to me from her balcony to let me know that the dog had given birth to six puppies.

'Not long after that I heard a radio report that a baby boy had been found dead and I had a feeling it involved her. I saw her later that day on the balcony again.

'She looked at me, I looked at her and she knew instantly that I knew the truth. From that day onwards I told her I wanted nothing more to do with her.'

Another neighbour revealed: 'She didn't seem to be too upset about her baby's death. In fact, she was going about her daily routine as though nothing had happened. When she was confronted about the baby's death she told people she hadn't laid a finger on her son.' Another noticed the smiling toddler: 'He was an adorable little boy with a wonderful smile. When I saw him a few months before he died, there didn't seem to be anything wrong. There were no marks on his body.

'Seeing his face in the newspapers and knowing what went on

breaks my heart. How could you hurt someone as innocent and trusting as that?'

How indeed? And what were the injuries that caused his death?

They were, in fact, so severe that they had to be computer generated onto a doll-like image to be shown at the subsequent trial.

As with the timetable of the dealings that the various authorities had with the child, to reduce Peter Connelly's life to a list seems a terrible thing to do. Yet only by listing the findings of the examination carried out after his death can anyone grasp the enormity of the damage caused to his tiny frame. Here are the post-mortem findings:

Weight at time of death 10.4kg (23lb)
Height 75.5cm (30in)
Damage to tip of middle finger and nail on right hand
Nail on right index finger damaged
Skin between lip and gum badly damaged
Bruising to right cheek
Damage to bridge of nose
An ulcerated lesion to the scalp
Bruising to forehead
Bruise to left temple
Bruising above left ear
Superficial abrasions on front of neck and beneath chin
Broken back
Superficial abrasions on front of neck and beneath chin
Irregularity of nails on left index and middle fingers

Bruising on lower back and lumbar spine
Bruises to left shin
Nail of right big toe missing, bruises behind toe
Bruising to right buttock
Eight fractured ribs
Bruises to chest

And that, according to Tracey Connelly, was 'a cot death.'

5

RUNNING FROM JUSTICE

EPPING FOREST is a narrow stretch of woodland that's 11 miles long, running from northeast London at one end to the Essex countryside at the other. Its Royal connections can be dated back almost 1,000 years to when Henry III gave it Royal status, and Henry VIII and Elizabeth I both hunted there in Tudor times.

Today, in addition to those who visit purely to enjoy its beauty, there is a host of other activities to take part in: running, horse riding, cycling and more. One activity not listed in any guide book, however, is the one that took Steven Barker, his brother Jason and Jason's 15-year-old girlfriend there in August 2007: 'Hiding.'

The trio decided to escape from Tottenham once little Peter's dead body had been taken from the house where he was tormented. They knew they would be wanted by police and so they decided to camp in the forest and hoped, by some bizarre reasoning, to escape capture. How long they planned to remain there it is hard to say, for surely even they must have known that the day of reckoning was at hand? As it transpired, their life 'on the run' lasted just 11 days before they were arrested.

The brothers had already tried to dispose of all the items of bloodstained bedding and clothing belonging to Peter, but they had one other piece of incriminating evidence to get rid of. A mobile phone containing images of Peter being abused was buried in woodland. Steven Barker was desperate to hide it as he was aware that it contained enough evidence to convict him, should the police ever discover the photographs and video images it contained, so the monster walked deep into the forest and buried it with his hands, scraping mud and earth from the dank floor to cover the hole he had made.

Barker's secret was revealed by the teenage girl, who was never charged over the incidents in the house, and who later told a friend: 'Steve used to laugh as he hit little Peter, he was so evil. He'd do horrible things to him and record it on his mobile phone. Peter would be crying and screaming, but Steve just used to laugh at him. He made me sick, but I was too scared of him to stop him.'

Barker and his elder brother took the girl with them to camp in the forest: 'That's when they went off into the woods to bury the phone,' she remembered.

Although Steven Barker was intimidated by his brother, it had not stopped him 'trying it on' with the youngster during the time they were all together. 'Steve was a monster with no regard for anyone. He was always trying it on with me,' she said. 'He kept touching me and brushing past me, even when Jason was in the same room; once he tried to force himself on me, it was horrible. I had to scream and scream to get him off.'

Although we have focussed so far on Steven Barker and Tracey Connelly, it would be wrong to regard Jason, who changed his surname to Owen by deed poll and tried to do so again while awaiting trial, as being an innocent party in all that happened. Indeed, he was far from it.

The pair were two of five children and their sister maintained the eldest boy Jason was the dominant one and he would bully his much larger, but younger brother. Steven Barker, in effect, confirmed this when he told police: 'There are lots of things I could tell you about Jason but I'm scared because I really believe he will try to have me killed.'

Big brother Jason, a former crack-cocaine addict, had arrived at the house in Tottenham in June 2007 with the teenage girl after splitting with his wife, the mother of his four children. He had convictions for arson – he set his home on fire to get re-housed – and burglary, and had been accused of rape when he was 13. Jason had also been investigated for victimising an Asian family and his move from south London to Tottenham was to escape the family of his 15-year-old lover.

But the trio couldn't even manage to 'disappear' efficiently and their life on the run came to an end when another camper in the woods reported them to police because he saw Steven Barker looking at his children from behind bushes; he had no idea Barker or his companions were wanted by detectives, of course, but the unusual behaviour of the younger brother alarmed him.

Only when their pictures were published over two years later, after all the names in the Baby P saga were made public, did he realise who he had been camping next to.

'If I hadn't stepped in, they could still be on the run now,' he said. 'I had no idea they were anything to do with Baby Peter – I was just protecting my kids. Our tent was pitched right next to theirs. I had no idea we were sleeping next to a pair of suspected killers sitting on a stash of weapons.

'I'm really relieved and a little bit proud of what I did that day. They are scum and I hope they never get out of prison.'

Days before, he noticed the threesome arriving on bikes with rucksacks and he confronted Barker: 'Someone told me a man was ducking around in the bushes, looking at my kids, so I went looking for him. He was stuttering and bumbling. I asked him where he was staying and he pointed at my tent so I knew straight away, he was lying.'

The man – a mechanic – even managed to squeeze 6ft 4in Barker's name out of him. When the elder brother and his lover returned to the site, they pretended they did not know Barker, then grabbed some things from their tent and left in a hurry.

'That made me certain he must be dodgy, so I called the police.' More than 20 officers with tracker dogs turned up, saying that Barker was wanted for burglary, and formally arrested him before searching for, and finding his brother and the girl.

With Connelly (who was by now expecting Steven Barker's child) and the Barker brothers in custody, the wheels of justice began to turn and soon they all appeared in court.

At the outset of the case there were no restrictions on identifying those involved and one national news agency report named all three, and Baby P in their report under the headline:

Pregnant Woman in Court on Baby Murder Charge

A pregnant woman appeared at the Old Bailey today charged with murdering her baby son. Tracey Connelly, 25 ... pleaded not guilty to murdering 17-month-old Peter Connelly on August 3. She also denied a charge of allowing or failing to prevent the death at her home in Penshurst Road, Tottenham, north London. Her partner Steven Barker, 31, of the same address, and his brother Jason Owen, 35, of Wittersham Road, Bromley, Kent, denied the same charges. Peter was pronounced dead at North Middlesex Hospital, north London, where he was taken with injuries. Connelly and Barker appeared in court by video link and were remanded in custody. Owen was granted conditional bail. And Judge Stephen Kramer set the trial date for June 9 next year.

Similar reports appeared on the BBC and on the Internet.

Indeed a national newspaper reported:

Tot Death Mum Has Baby

A young mum awaiting trial for killing her 17-month-old son has given birth to a second child. Tracey Connelly, 26, had her daughter taken off her immediately by police and social services and was returned to jail from hospital just hours later.

She denies murdering her son Peter, who died from injuries including a broken back and eight broken ribs last August. A source said: "She was under guard. Police stated that under no circumstances could she have contact with the baby." Her partner Steven Barker, 31, of Tottenham, North London, denies murder and both also deny allowing or failing to prevent Peter's death. They are due for trial in June.

In fact, the trial was put back until September 2008 after an application from the defence and by the opening day of the case, the 9th of that month, the restrictions on identifying many of those involved were in place.

Nevertheless, the gravity of the charge facing the three and the death of such a young child guaranteed coverage in the Press.

The jury were told the facts that were soon to be ingrained in the nation's conscience: how Baby P, as he was now to be called, had his back broken as the climax of eight months of violence leading to his death even though he had been placed on Haringey Council's Child Protection Register months before he died, and that the mother and her partner – neither publicly named – were on police bail after being arrested on suspicion of assaulting the child before his death.

Doctors and social workers had seen the toddler in the run-up to his death, the court learned. They feared that the mother could neglect and physically abuse the baby.

Yet 'Baby P' was still returned to his mother and died in circumstances which would be 'likely to fill any reasonable person with revulsion', the court heard.

For the first time the injuries he suffered, including those already referred to in this book, were revealed to the wider world. The jury learned of his eight fractured ribs, the broken tooth he had swallowed, the missing fingertips and fingernails, the ulcerated cuts on his scalp and the torn lips and gums. And of course, there was that terrible, terrible broken back.

Sally O'Neill QC, prosecuting said: 'That particular injury requires an extremely forceful hyper-extension of the spine by, for example, forcing a child's back over your bent knee or over a banister rail. The effect of that particular assault would have been to cause paralysis from the level of the injury down.'

The prosecutor added that the baby's mother took P to the Child Development Centre to assess his development two days before his death and Baby P was seen by Dr Sabah Al-Zayyat, a locum consultant paediatrician, who noted a number of bruises but decided not to give him a full systemic examination because P was 'miserable and cranky.'

Yet many of the injuries P suffered – including the fractured ribs and the paralysis from the spine injury – were caused at least 48 hours before his death. 'This would have been evidenced at the very least by floppiness and could not fail to have been observed by a competent doctor who had examined P properly,' said Miss O'Neill.

A child being 'miserable and cranky may not seem to you or me to be the best reason for a consultant paediatrician to not fully examine a child who is known to be on the Child Protection Register,' she added. The prosecutor also told the jury that there were 'some unsatisfactory features' in the doctor's evidence, including alterations to her notes after P died, a few days after.

Connelly and Steven Barker, both unidentified to the world at large, and defendant Jason Owen all pleaded not guilty to murdering Baby P and an alternative count of causing or allowing his death.

All three in the dock said they knew nothing of the injuries inflicted on P or 'that one of their co-defendants was responsible,' the court was told.

'Whether they inflicted the injuries themselves or knew that one of their co-defendants was doing so, either way they knew what was going on and were a party to these unlawful assaults – the effects of which over the last few days in particular would have been absolutely clear to any adult in the house,' said Miss O'Neill.

The prosecutor gave details of Connelly's marriage and subsequent meeting with Barker and her husband's departure from the marital home and provided a timetable of Peter's injuries, saying his mother appeared 'flustered and unable to provide a clear explanation' of his injuries when Peter was admitted to the Whittington Hospital, the mother claiming his bruises were caused by falling off a settee onto toys and that the scratches had come from their dog. She told doctors that her boyfriend came to the house but was never left with the child on his own. 'This was not accurate but was an untruth which was persisted in throughout. You may want to consider whether it is a significant one,' said Miss O'Neill.

On 30 October, both Connelly and Jason Owen were found not guilty of Peter's murder on the judge's direction.

Judge Kramer said: 'After hearing submissions I have decided as a matter of law there is insufficient evidence against Tracey Connelly and Jason Owen for the case against them to continue.'

Steven Barker still faced charges of murder and causing or allowing the death of a child while Jason Owen continued to face charges of causing or allowing the death of a child. Previously, Connelly had pleaded guilty to causing or allowing the death of her child.

Beginning her summing-up, Miss O'Neill said: 'The spotlight turns entirely on the boyfriend as the person who carried out these acts. We submit that Baby P was unlawfully killed and that the two defendants you are concerned with were involved in an immediate clean-up as soon as Baby P had gone from the premises and before the 999 call was made, as far as his clothing was concerned.'

It was not until 11 November that the verdicts were reached on the two men: Steven Barker was found not guilty of murder but he and his brother were found guilty of causing or allowing the death of a child, the charge Connelly had already admitted.

Judge Stephen Kramer excused the jury from further service for 10 years, saying: 'You have heard evidence of a harrowing nature and you have seen things which in the course of your everyday life you would not be expected to see.'

None of the evil three were sentenced that day, but it made no difference. With their verdicts now given, all hell was about to break loose.

6

FAILINGS &
RECRIMINATIONS

SADLY, the storm about to break over the heads of Haringey Council and its staff wasn't the first time that the local authority had been involved in the death of a helpless child.

At the time of the first death there had been action to prevent such a tragedy happening again and yet here it was repeating itself: a combination of wrong decisions and lack of communication, all with the result that a child's life was lost.

At the beginning of this book we looked at the area's social problems and how the local authority was forced to cope with them. The fact of the matter was that now, with the Baby P case, Haringey would forever be labelled in many people's minds as 'The council that lets children die'. Of course children died elsewhere in the country, yet it was Haringey that was now synonymous with avoidable infant death.

In the late 1990s the Labour-run council had far fewer social workers than were needed to deal with vulnerable children, critics stated, because money was instead being spent on vote-winning education improvements, a state of affairs which came to light after the death of the other child who will be eternally linked with the council, Victoria Climbie.

The 8-year-old girl from the Ivory Coast died in January 2000 after being beaten, starved and tortured by her great-aunt, Marie Thérèse Kouao and Kouao's boyfriend, Carl Manning. The little girl had been seen several times by Haringey's social workers, as well as by hospital staff and police, but because of what a judge described as 'blinding incompetence', her suffering and subsequent death occurred, despite at least 12 opportunities to save her.

The public inquiry held by Lord Laming into Victoria Climbie's death heard how the junior social worker assigned to her case, Lisa Arthurworrey, had been given too many files to work on while her supervisor herself had a child of her own taken into care and had been found unfit to do her job. Miss Arthurworrey was later sacked and banned from social work but a tribunal claimed she had also been a 'victim' of the tragedy and she was allowed to return to social work.

The council's Social Services department was subsequently given a 'no-star' rating and placed in special measures when the Department of Health introduced its monitoring scheme in 2002.

There is no doubt that Baby P's death would have attracted attention no matter where it occurred – the death of a child whose welfare was the concern of the local authority is, and always should be, a cause of genuine concern and public debate. Decent society wouldn't have it any other way. But the Haringey connection served to emphasise the tragedy of Peter's death and the ways in which it could, and should, have been avoided.

To that end, the council sought to explain its role in the case in what was to become a matter of controversy. They held a press briefing to coincide with the end of the trial to put their side of the story only for it to become 'a complete disaster' in the words of one woman official. That official was Sharon Shoesmith, at the time the £100,000-a-year head of the council's Children's department, who was about to become a central figure in the case.

Her presentation of the council's views immediately brought widespread criticism for failing to apologise for their role in the life and death of Baby P. One observer even went so far as to say: 'Her words will long be remembered as the most inflammatory – and insensitive – of any utterances by a public servant, certainly one in charge of protecting children.'

What the Irish-born, 55-year-old said was: 'The child was killed by members of his own family and not by Social Services. The very sad fact is that we can't stop people who are determined to kill children.' It was a remark that left her wide open to attack, and it duly came. Some months later, she eventually explained the reasoning behind that briefing and put her side of the story, but there is no doubt that the overall impression left at the time was a disastrous one.

During a Press conference she presented seven graphs aimed at showing her department's progress and said it had 'three-star' services, a reference to its council performance rating. The graphs showed how many children in care achieved GCSE results, how many were adopted and how many received various health and welfare check-ups within recommended timescales. Haringey held the briefing at a four-star London hotel, where it had hired at least three rooms.

The council also spent £19,000 of public money on media training in preparation for the briefing, another matter that angered critics.

It wasn't just the national press and television who were critical of the council's attitude, though – the influential magazine *PR Week* quoted one crisis management expert as saying, 'The first quote from the woman was, "You can't stop people from killing their children." I thought what an incredibly naive thing to say. It is bog-standard crisis communications – the first thing you do is you acknowledge that something has gone wrong.'

The use of graphs and charts was also criticised. 'Speak in the same language. If people are talking in emotional terms, do not reel out charts, graphs and status reports.'

The mother of two grown-up daughters, Shoesmith was raised in County Antrim and after a spell as a school teacher became a government education inspector and then moved on to become education director in Haringey before taking up her current job.

Ironically, she became the head of Haringey's Children's Services, which covers both education and social services because of the changes in the way councils run child protection, ordered by the Government after the report by Lord Laming into Victoria Climbie's death. He said that teachers and social workers should co-operate more closely so that no child at risk of being hurt or abused ever slipped through the net again.

Public anger grew when it emerged that no one at Haringey had resigned or been sacked over the case. Shoesmith chaired the council's Local Safeguarding Children Board (LSCB), which conducted an internal inquiry into the case. According to her, 'There was not the evidence there for anyone to lose their jobs.'

Indeed, the only action taken against staff was three written warnings.

The fact that Shoesmith was in charge of an inquiry into events which were linked to her own staff was also widely criticised, although she later pointed out this was normal procedure elsewhere in the country. But there was nothing that could be done to stop the anger over the case: this wasn't just a media storm either – it also became political dynamite.

Conservative Party leader David Cameron was among those asking questions over the case and called for sackings over the council's failure to save Baby P. The Tory leader said he was 'sickened to the core' by the crime and further angered by the lack of a proper apology.

In a strong attack on the council officials and others responsible for the child's care, Mr Cameron condemned Haringey's decision to respond by issuing written warnings to three staff as inadequate, saying, 'Those whose job it was to oversee this system have failed. They must admit that and pay a price. Society cannot work unless individuals carry the consequence of their actions.

'We've had a raft of excuses and not one apology. Everyone says that they followed protocol to the letter and that the fault lies with systemic failure. But we cannot allow the words 'systemic failure' to absolve anyone of any responsibility. Systems are made up of people and the buck has got to stop somewhere.'

Although Government ministers had announced a nationwide

review of child protection procedures, Mr Cameron said that while policy changes should be examined, they should not be allowed to obscure the need for those responsible for Baby P to answer for their failures. He added: 'There'll be lots of talk now about resources and coordination, reviews and procedures and yes, these things are important. But let's be frank – this child was seen not once, not twice, but 60 times. The whistle should have been blown, the child should have been taken into care, the repeated cruelty should have been stopped... It's about responsibility, not just in procedure and protocol.'

Director of the Victoria Climbie Foundation, Mr Mor Dioum, commented: 'For no one to take responsibility for the lost opportunities to save Baby P is a betrayal of him and everyone who relies on these people. Someone must be made accountable for the systematic failures which allowed him to die. We must be careful not to simply scapegoat frontline staff.

'We need to look to the people who were actually in charge – they need to take responsibility. The lessons of Victoria Climbie's death have not been learned, even in the borough where she died. We must have a public inquiry that looks at the mistakes made by people at the top of Haringey council and other organisations.'

Children's Minister Beverley Hughes added to the pressure on Haringey Council when she called on its chief executive and councillors to look at whether senior officials should be held accountable for the death: 'I think the council has a responsibility; it is an elected body, it has the responsibility to ask itself the question, in the light of this case, whether there is an accountability at another level in the management of this case,' she said, and described the decisions made as 'very, very wrong' as she demanded further investigation of the local authority responsible.

Announcing the independent review of Child Protection Services, Hughes stated: 'To ensure that the reforms the government set out following Lord Laming's inquiry are being implemented systematically, Ed Balls and I have today asked Lord Laming to prepare an independent report of progress being made across the country.'

Lord Laming, who called for a series of reforms following the Climbie tragedy, had been asked by Ms Hughes to prepare an independent report into the implementation of his reforms across the country. He told one interviewer: 'It would be awful wherever it happened, but it seems particularly sad that it happened in the same area where Victoria experienced this awful cruelty and a terrible death, and involved the very same services.

He added, 'What we know about people who deliberately harm children is that they go to great lengths to disguise their activities. People who work in this field have to be streetwise and they certainly have to be sceptical. They have to make sure that all the activities are monitored, that the child is regularly seen and that they observe the way in which child and parents relate to each other.'

While interviewing Ms Hughes, GMTV presenter Ben Shephard remarked on the statement by Sharon Shoesmith that, 'the very sad fact is that we can't stop people who are determined to kill children' showed 'complete apathy' and was 'despicable', adding, 'That is exactly what they should be able to do.' Ms Hughes replied: 'I think that is right, in a case like this... and this is the difference with Victoria Climbie largely, where it was known the child was being injured, the child was on the Child Protection Register, all the agencies – unlike in the Victoria Climbie case – were working together.

'Now it is unacceptable that in a case like that, we can't say that we can protect children; that is unacceptable. That is why I have asked Lord Laming to give me a view as to what the situation is like in terms of progress of implementing his report across the country. It is why I have also said I am looking personally into the case of Haringey. I think what has happened there does need further examination.'

She added that the system had been applied 'properly' in the case, but the way in which it was implemented and the decisions made were clearly wrong.

Lib Dem MP for Hornsey and Wood Green, Lynne Featherstone commented that the child fell through 'safety net after safety net' and called for an independent investigation by the Children's Commissioner. 'The Children's Act was borne out of tragedy in Haringey after the death of Victoria Climbie,' she said. 'Yet eight years after her death, the law created to stop this happening again has failed to prevent a similar tragedy in the same borough.'

She also called for Sharon Shoesmith and the council cabinet member for Children's Services, Liz Santry, to resign or be sacked, saying: 'The legislation puts the director and cabinet member in the frame. No one was sacked or resigned last time and that is why this has happened again. This time, heads must roll.'

Liberal Democrat Leader Nick Clegg remarked: 'This is a

shocking tragedy which must now lead to a fully independent investigation by the Children's Commissioner into what went so terribly wrong. Eight years after the death of Victoria Climbie, the law created to stop this happening again has failed. Clearly all the circumstances must be examined again thoroughly.'

At a local level, Robert Gorrie, Lib Dem leader of the opposition at Haringey Council, said: 'Closed-door reviews by the council are completely inadequate. The credibility of Haringey's child protection system has been called into question again.'

It emerged that Dr Sabah Al-Zayyat, the Great Ormond Street doctor who missed the baby's broken back, had not had her contract renewed and was appealing against the decision. Dr Jane Collins, chief executive of the hospital, said: 'It is clear that more should have been done when the child was seen by a paediatrician two days before the child died.'

NSPCC acting chief executive Wes Cuell observed that professionals dedicated to protecting children were 'overwhelmed' by the scale of child abuse and supporting them must be a priority for the Government.

The Schools and Families Secretary, Ed Balls, said that the review of the case already conducted by the council indicated major failures, poor management and inappropriate actions on the part of the agencies involved in the north London borough of Haringey. In a damning summary of the review, Balls said that, 'Each agency has singly and collectively failed to adhere to the procedures for the proper management of child protection cases.'

As a result, he had ordered an inquiry under the Children Act into the safeguarding of children in Haringey. It would be conducted by Ofsted, the Commission for Healthcare Audit and Inspection and the Chief Inspector of Constabulary.

'The review will need to undertake an urgent and thorough inspection of the quality of practice and management of all services which contribute to the effective safeguarding of children in the local area,' he said.

He added that the staff concerned had failed to follow the correct practices set out in Working Together 2006, the guide produced by the government for such cases. Balls said that there might be other areas where, if proper procedures had been followed, then it, 'could have led to a better outcome for the child.'

'The death of Baby P in Haringey is a very tragic case that will have shocked and appalled the country,' said Balls. 'It makes all of us question how someone could do such a terrible thing to a child and set out to deceive the very people trying to help.'

He said the Serious Case Review handed to him that morning showed that agencies in Haringey had, 'singly and collectively failed to adhere to the procedures for the proper management of child protection cases.'

There was evidence of 'poor-quality practice, management and supervision of staff in all agencies'. Health professionals, 'appear to have failed to follow the appropriate procedures when there was evidence of a child having suffered non-accidental injuries'.

Then there was 'inappropriate use of family friends as temporary carers for Baby P'.

Mr Balls said: 'Clearly such findings in an individual case

raise serious concerns about the wider systems and management of services for safeguarding children in Haringey.'

The findings prompted his decision to order the urgent Joint Area Review of safeguarding and promoting the welfare of children in Haringey, which would issue an initial report by 1 December, he confirmed.

Meanwhile, the director of children's services in Hampshire, John Coughlan, had been immediately drafted in to work alongside his counterpart in Haringey to ensure proper procedures for safeguarding children were in place and properly applied while the inquiry took place.

Barry Sheerman, chairman of the House of Commons Children's, Schools and Families select committee, said he believed the existing legislative framework should be re-examined; one reason for the concern being that Haringey twice sought legal advice about taking Baby P into care – and twice were told that the legal threshold for going to court to obtain a care order had not been met.

Liz Santry welcomed the new inquiry and said the council was itself commissioning an independent expert to lead a cross-party review of Child Protection in the borough.

'We recognise that the people of Haringey must have full confidence in the support we provide to those who cannot support themselves,' she commented. 'If any further recommendations arise over the coming weeks, we will not hesitate to act on them. We want our Child Protection to be the very best possible.'

Shadow children's secretary Michael Gove welcomed the Government's announcement of an inquiry: 'The situation in

Haringey clearly requires the most expert independent figures from outside to investigate and make recommendations. It's crucial we learn lessons as quickly as possible to avert future tragedies.'

Lynne Featherstone added further to the debate when she remarked: 'The leader of Haringey Council was the leader of Haringey Council when Victoria was killed so definitely, I think there should be political responsibility and political heads on the line because, unless and until jobs are on the line in this sort of dreadful, tragic situation, I don't believe that those people will ensure the recommendations are carried out in full.'

The announcement by Mr Balls of the Independent Inquiry was preceded by one of the most astonishing rows the House of Commons had seen in years. Some commentators even suggested the announcement might have been prompted by the fact that Prime Minister Gordon Brown did not come over well during the debate during Prime Minister's Question Time with David Cameron.

Either way, the stormy discussion was labelled 'politics at its worst' by one writer while veteran commentator Simon Hoggart, writing in the *Guardian*, described it thus:

Ghastly, embarrassing, shameful. As they discussed the case of the tortured and mutilated Baby P, you could almost see the baby's body hurled from one side to another. We're always hearing about political footballs. This was a political corpse.

'I don't think anybody meant it to end up like this way. It was like a spat at a funeral. Emotions are raw, festering resentments come to the surface, and before you know it, members of the family are thrashing out, wrestling each other into the grave, then wondering in horror what on earth had come over them.

It would have been all too easy for one side or another to back down. As it is, the nation was forced to witness the degrading sight of its elected representatives trying to seize the advantage in a case that appalled everyone who heard of it.

Things began quietly. David Cameron wanted to know why the inquiry in Haringey was being conducted by Sharon Shoesmith, head of the very department under whose surveillance the death occurred.

The Prime Minister declined to answer.

So what exactly had ignited emotions to such a remarkable extent? The goings-on in that sordid Tottenham house now entered centre stage of the Mother of Parliaments and were reported around the world. A full account is needed to illustrate the depth of feeling that day in the Commons.

Mr Brown said the tragic death, 'raises serious questions that we have to address' and promised the Government would take action after receiving a report that day from Haringey Council, which identified 'weaknesses' in procedures, but opposition leader Mr Cameron said the local review could not possibly be undertaken by the council's own children's services director.

The exchanges then descended into a fierce row after Mr Brown said he regretted the opposition leader making a 'party political' issue of the tragic case. Conservative MPs loudly shouted 'cheap!' and 'shameful!' at the Prime Minister and the then Speaker Michael Martin was forced to repeatedly intervene, appealing for both sides to be quiet and let the two party leaders speak.

Mr Cameron then labelled Mr Brown's remark 'cheap' and demanded he withdraw it, having asked 'perfectly reasonable' questions about the case. Mr Brown refused to do so, insisting instead that it was right to maximise agreement on this 'sad and tragic case'. The Government had acted immediately in the aftermath of the court case. What mattered was the protection of young children, he added.

Mr Cameron was visibly angry about the Prime Minister's response to his questions, repeatedly stabbing the despatch box with his finger as he made his points and even sent his papers flying to the floor.

The exchanges in the Commons at Question Time began routinely, but relations between Mr Brown and Mr Cameron appeared to quickly sink to new depths. The Tory leader said: 'I want to ask about the tragic death of Baby P. This happened in the same children's services department that was responsible for Victoria Climbie and yet again nobody is taking responsibility, nobody has resigned.

'Do you agree with me that the Haringey Inquiry is completely unacceptable? It is being led by Mrs Shoesmith, who is the council's own director of children's services. Do you agree with me she cannot possibly investigate the failure of her own department?'

Mr Brown replied: 'I believe I speak for the whole country when I say that people are not only shocked and saddened, but horrified and angered by what they have seen reported about what happened to an innocent 17-month-old boy. Every child is precious and every child is unique. Every child should have the benefit of support and protection, both from their parents and the authorities that be. This tragedy that has arisen because of the violence and torture of a young child, where three have already been found guilty, raises serious questions we have to address.

'The first set of questions is being addressed by Lord Laming, who is now looking at Social Service Protection for children in every part of the country. He did the Victoria Climbie Inquiry. His recommendations were accepted by all parties in this House as being necessary and he will now look at what needs to be done.

'The second issue is in Haringey itself. There is a serious case review. The executive report already says there have been failings and weaknesses in the system. The full report has now arrived with the Children's Secretary [Ed Balls] this morning. It is now for the Government to take action and we will make a decision about what procedures and processes we will adopt in relation to Haringey.

'I believe that is the right thing to do – both local review and national action.'

Mr Cameron continued: 'May I ask again about the local review, Sharon Shoesmith, who is carrying this out...' Though Labour MPs protested loudly, he persisted, 'MPs should worry about this. This is a local authority that has completely failed. What she said is that her service had "worked effectively". The Children's Minister said recently that many areas set up their safeguarding board with the local director of children's services as the chair, that is something frankly that does concern me. So, isn't it unacceptable that the person who runs the children's services department is responsible for looking into what her own department did?'

Mr Brown said procedures created after Lord Laming's previous inquiry meant the local authority director of children's services and local members had to accept their responsibility. The Government created local safeguarding children's boards.

'When an incident like this happens, which is so tragic, a report has to be done. That report is submitted to the Children's Secretary. The report has arrived on his desk this morning. We've already got the executive summary, which was published yesterday, which identified weaknesses in the system.

'The decision will then be made about what to do in relation to Haringey and what procedures have to be followed. I do believe there was all-party support for the Laming report when it was done and this is the right way forward.'

With the temperature rising, Mr Cameron replied: 'I asked a straightforward question and there's absolutely no answer.'

Amid more noise from the Labour benches, Mr Martin intervened, saying: 'Please let Mr Cameron be heard. It will not do [to have] shouting across the chamber after this terrible news has come to us. It's best to let him speak.'

Mr Cameron went on: 'I'll tell you what is shameful and that is trying to shout down someone who's asking reasonable questions about something that's gone wrong.'

He said: 'Let's be honest. This is a story about a 17-year-old girl who had no idea how to bring up a child. It's about a boyfriend who couldn't read, but could beat a child and it's about a Social Services department that gets £100 million a year and can't look after children.

'In the case of failing schools, we take them over. This department in Haringey, one in four positions for social workers is completely vacant. They do nothing to help struggling local schools that are failing and another child has been beaten to death.

'Will you – I don't expect an answer now, you never get one – at least consider whether the time has come to take over this failing department and put someone in charge who can run it properly for our children?'

Mr Brown replied: 'I think we are both agreed this is a tragic and serious loss of life that has got to be investigated properly so that all the lessons can be learned. I think you would agree that appointing Lord Laming to go round the country, to look at what is happening in each area... is the right thing to do.

'I think you have got to accept that the executive summary already published shows that there are weaknesses that exist. So there is an admission of weaknesses that have got to be addressed. We have received the full report this morning. We will act on it quickly. We will do it in the right way so that we come to the judgments that are necessary to protect children in the future.

'I do regret making a party political issue of this issue. I do regret that because I think...' Mr Brown was drowned out by Opposition protests, but Mr Martin said the Prime Minister was in order. The Prime Minister continued '...because I think the whole country shares the outrage, the whole country wants to see action and the whole country will support the action that is being taken nationally, and in relation to Haringey.'

Mr Cameron came back again, telling the Prime Minister: 'I

think what you said just now is frankly cheap. I asked some perfectly reasonable questions about a process that is wrong and I would ask you to withdraw the attack that that was about party politics.'

Mr Brown told him: 'There is common ground on both sides of the House and we should maximise our agreement on these issues about this very sad and tragic case. We have taken action immediately to set up an Independent Inquiry. That Independent Inquiry under Lord Laming is one I believe all people will support.

'Action is going to be taken in relation to Haringey because we have just received the full report and the executive summary has already identified weaknesses. We have acted immediately after the end of the court case and we will continue to take action because what really matters is the protection of young children in every part of the country.'

Mr Cameron retorted: 'You accused me of party politics...'

But a fresh wave of protests from the Labour benches brought the Speaker to his feet again.

'I appeal to the House again. It is not a good thing at this time when we have heard this news about a little child that we should be shouting across the chamber. Let the leader of the Opposition speak and also the Prime Minister.'

Mr Cameron said: 'All I'm asking is that you accused me of party politics. I did not mention who runs this council, or who ran it when Victoria Climbie was tragically killed. All I asked for is that you withdraw your accusation that in any way I was playing party politics and not asking a perfectly reasonable question about a tragic case. I ask one more time: please just withdraw that I was playing party politics. You know I wasn't.'

But Mr Brown refused to be drawn, saying, to shouts of 'withdraw' from the Tory benches: 'I think the whole House will now want to find unity around these three things. First of all that this tragic incident has got to be investigated in every possible way. Secondly, that the Lord Laming review is the right inquiry to have and thirdly, now that the case review has arrived with the Children's Secretary, he will take the action that is necessary. I hope the whole House can agree these are the right things and we are doing the right things to get the right answer.'

Mr Cameron responded: 'Obviously you don't feel able to withdraw what you said. Let me just ask one more time on the central point, which doesn't just apply in Haringey, but which may well be a problem elsewhere as your own Children's Minister has said – that we have a system that allows directors of children's services to examine the conduct of their own department. This is wrong in every other walk of life. This must be wrong in Social Services, where we are dealing with the most difficult and sensitive decisions.

'So will you at least take away what your children's spokesman has said and say you should not investigate your own conduct. It's simple. Give a pledge?'

Mr Brown said: 'I'm sorry you don't recognise that the action we have taken has been immediately after the court case.' He continued to repeat: 'We have set up the Independent Inquiry under Lord Laming. We have the report this morning on the case review; that report will be acted on immediately.

'Surely it is in the interests of all of us to think of a young child and what we can do to make sure this doesn't ever happen again.'

Lynne Featherstone then told MPs she was Leader of the Opposition on Haringey Council at the time of the Victoria Climbie case and was told, 'lessons would be learned'. Ms Featherstone said the report commissioned by the Government into Baby P did not 'go far enough'.

She told Mr Brown: 'Whilst I welcome your announcement yesterday, that Lord Laming will lead a national review of Child Protection Services, in terms of Haringey it doesn't go far enough.

'And while I hear what you say about looking at the report, that is not a report that will guarantee the safety of children in my borough. So I would ask you – look at that report, but call for an Independent Public Inquiry.'

Referring to Mr Cameron's previous comments, Mr Brown told Ms Featherstone: 'I'm grateful for the way you have put the set of issues that have got to be addressed.'

He continued: 'The first set of issues that have got to be addressed is can we ensure the protection of children following the Laming report after the Victoria Climbie case in all parts of the country? And that we are determined to do.

'The second set of issues arises in Haringey itself and the executive summary has already pointed to weaknesses in what is done there and that is why the Secretary for Children has received the report this morning, which is now the full report.

'He will take as quick action on that as is necessary and look at the procedures that need to be followed in Haringey itself.'

Another commentator on the political scene wrote the next day of, 'An incredible display of anger, emotion, bitterness, shameless politicking and a Prime Minister too embarrassed to admit he was out of order.'

It had been an astonishing scene and one described here in detail to show the depth of feeling of all who become immersed in the case. Indeed, it wasn't long before Haringey Council also finally announced its 'deepest sorrow' at Peter's death. It had only taken a couple of days, but it seemed like an eternity.

Liz Santry, Haringey Council cabinet member for children and young people, promised complete cooperation: 'On behalf of Haringey Council I would like to say how deeply saddened I am about the death of Baby P. He died over 15 months ago, and for those past months in Haringey there has been a huge amount of anguish, and endless discussion about what more we might have done. I have to say that we are truly sorry that we did not do more to protect him.'

In a statement on the council website that day, she said the authority had been 'devastated' by the death of Baby P. Santry welcomed Ed Balls' review, saying the council would cooperate fully and that it had, 'moved swiftly after the death of Baby P to check our Child Protection procedures, and strengthen them, where necessary.'

'We are truly sorry that we did not do more to protect him,' she told Sky News. She said the council was commissioning an independent expert, 'to review the actions taken by our staff and the member oversight of Child Protection in the borough. If any further recommendations arise over the coming weeks we will not hesitate to act on them. We want our Child Protection to be the very best possible.'

Balls, meanwhile, said that he would not prejudge the work of inspectors, who would report on the care of children in Haringey by 1 December. He was prepared to act, however, if they identified problems: 'These are really difficult jobs, but in the end, if there are management systemic failures, then yes, there has got to be accountability and also there has to be action to make sure things are put right. I have the powers to act, but I am not going to do the easy political thing and seek a headline with an action today. I want to do it properly and that's why the inspectors are doing it. In the end, if there are failures, there has got to be accountability.'

In extreme circumstances Balls could impose new managers to take over the running of the council's Children's Services department. The children's secretary said that the review of the case already conducted by the council indicated major failures, poor management and inappropriate actions on the part of the agencies involved in the north London borough.

But if anyone thought this might bring a temporary end to the shockwaves and recriminations resulting from the case, they were to be proved wrong in a very short space of time.

7

THE WHISTLEBLOWER

THE ECHOES of the astonishing row between the Prime Minister and the Leader of the Opposition could still be heard when another development shed more light on life within the troubled Haringey Council.

It emerged that six months before Baby P died, former Haringey social worker Nevres Kemal wrote to Patricia Hewitt, the then Health Secretary, and three other ministers to highlight Haringey's inadequacies in dealing with abuse claims. She asked for a Public Inquiry on the grounds that, 'Child abusers are not being tackled.'

The letters had been sent on her behalf by her solicitor Lawrence Davies in February 2007: Ms Kemal had been working on a different case in which children from one family were being sexually abused by a relative. She said the council had failed to act on her information and that she was dismissed for causing trouble.

The letter was sent to Ms Hewitt, the then culture minister David Lammy and junior health ministers Rosie Winterton and

Ivan Lewis. Mr Lewis was also responsible for the Department of Health's Social-Care portfolio.

It read: 'Our client whistle-blew the fact that the sexual abuse had been ongoing for months and the new management brought in post-Climbie had not acted... We write to ask for a public inquiry into these matters.'

Kemal's solicitor received a reply from the Government informing him that it would not undertake an inquiry. He was quoted as saying: 'Ms Kemal spotted the flaws at Haringey Council, exactly the same flaws as the ones that allowed Victoria Climbie to die and Baby P to die. We asked for a public inquiry. Who knows what could have been done if they had undertaken one? It's just tragic.'

The letter was also sent to the Department of Health's Commission for Social Care Inspection – the watchdog body for social workers. Again, the query was passed between departments, but no action was taken. Mr Davies added, 'The Social Care Inspectorate are the people with the hit squads, if they are tipped off about things like this. It is their job to investigate but they didn't. Why?'

Ms Kemal's allegations first came to light at an employment tribunal in 2007. She claimed the council's inaction had exposed children in the same family to the risk of sexual abuse by a relative. This was four years after Lord Laming published his report into the death of Victoria Climbie and she stated that procedural recommendations set out in that report were not being followed.

The Department for Children, Schools and Families confirmed it had received the letter 21 months ago. A spokeswoman said:

'Our records show we received a letter dated 16 February 2007, forwarded to us from the Department of Health, detailing an employment tribunal issue with Haringey Council, and containing an allegation that Child Protection procedures were not being followed in Haringey. Officials from this department replied on 21 March 2007. In that letter they made the point that ministers could not comment on the specific details of the employment tribunal case. As is standard practice, they suggested that the individual should notify the relevant Inspectorate, the Commission for Social Care Inspection, to take appropriate action and they provided the necessary contact details.'

Kemal's lawyer, Mr Davies said that his client's concerns had been 'pushed from pillar to post' and suggested Baby P's death might have been averted, had they been acted upon.

That weekend Ms Kemal, 44, was quoted in two national newspapers on her concerns about Child Care in Haringey.

'My life has been ruined and I have never worked since,' she told the *Daily Mail*. 'My family has been through hell. But I tell you this, if I had to do it all again, I would do it, for the sake of the children in Haringey. From the moment I walked into Haringey Council, I felt something was wrong. We were bombarded with too many cases and there were too few social workers to cope. There are thousands of vulnerable children in Haringey who cannot defend themselves. I felt that something was going to happen. I have had to speak out.'

Kemal, who had 14 years as a child protection officer behind her, was hired in the August of 2004 as a £38,000-a-year social worker at the council: 'I knew that Haringey was not a popular council to work for and that the death of Victoria Climbie meant a lot of social workers didn't want to go there, but I thought I could do some good. I just hoped to do my job and make sure that children were protected.'

In the autumn of that year she claimed that seven children, aged between three and 16, who suffered physical and sexual abuse by a relative, were left with their attacker for nine months before being taken into care.

The *Mail* pointed out that she '...is barred by an injunction and a gagging order from talking in any detail about her work with children in Haringey. But before the draconian rulings to silence her were imposed, she said what she repeats now.'

Kemal continued: 'The case of the seven children was like Climbie all over again, except that thankfully on this occasion no child actually died. But the system at the council had failed, and children's lives were being put at risk.'

Of the letters that had been sent in February, she commented to the *Mail*: 'No one listened to me. If ministers had acted on what I told them then – perhaps – this Baby P might still be alive. The frightening thing is that after I voiced my fears, I was immediately victimised. They tried to trip me up. When that didn't work, they made false accusations against me. Everything I know, I want to tell the Government, so no other child dies like Victoria Climbie or Baby P.'

Indeed, she spoke at even greater length to the *Mail's* sister paper, the *Mail On Sunday*, the next day, where she was quoted as saying that after being falsely accused of waving a fist at a young girl – which, according to Haringey, constituted 'child abuse' – 'They then turned their attention to my own daughter and launched a child protection investigation into her, which means that they felt she was at risk. Ultimately, it could have led to her being taken away from me. I felt terribly frightened all the time. It was evil.' Ms Kemal then described how she faced a four-year 'witch-hunt', during which she lost her job, faced a police investigation and saw her family and health fall apart.

An employment tribunal heard that she had been singled out for being a whistleblower. Haringey eventually dropped the case and paid her undisclosed compensation, the paper reported.

It continued by quoting her as saying, 'God save us from endless inquiries. What Haringey needs is managers sacked and arrested, commonsense to prevail and money put into frontline services.'

Children's Services Director Sharon Shoesmith and Deputy Director Cecilia Hitchen subsequently agreed in writing that Miss Kemal had never abused a child, in or outside of work, added the *Mail On Sunday*.

'The office was very cliquey. Two key senior women were in a relationship, and if your face didn't fit, that was it. You'd just be handed files, with no discussion. If you asked questions, you were stupid,' Kemal added. She said that of the 20 or so who worked in her open-plan office, most were agency staff or newly-qualified Jamaican social workers, brought to Britain by Haringey on costly relocation packages.

Kemal was concerned in October 2004 when she was handed a case in which teachers and relatives feared a male carer had subjected children to serious abuse and had alerted Social Services to the situation many months before. However, the social worker responsible had quit, the file had not been reallocated and the children were simply forgotten.

She told a subsequent industrial tribunal: 'Children had not been properly protected. It was exactly the sort of situation, after the mistakes of the Victoria Climbie tragedy in Haringey, that the new management brought in to improve procedures and standards in child protection was supposed to prevent.'

In November 2004, she managed to get the children added to the Child Protection Register and they were eventually taken into care: 'But after this whistleblowing, management became hostile towards me. I was destructively and comprehensively investigated and punished for doing nothing wrong, whereas the managers who investigated me left children with an abuser for months. It was Climbie all over again, except that thankfully on this occasion no child died.'

Subsequently she was involved in a length dispute with the council over her alleged behaviour towards a teenage girl during a row at the house of a family acquaintance. Kemal says she raised her voice to be heard above the noise and held her hand up in a 'stop' gesture to the girl. This led to a complaint from one of the girl's family

Kemal was suspended and a full-scale child abuse investigation was launched, which meant the council could turn their attention towards Kemal's own daughter, 13 at the time. On this, she said: 'I reacted like normal families react – with anger and disbelief. What was so terribly wrong is that a system that had the power and the duty to protect children was now hounding me for trying to protect children. It was like I was in a fascist country. I felt totally alone.'

In January 2005 police arrived at Kemal's home and cautioned her over the alleged common assault, but days later told Social

Services there were no grounds for prosecution. Indeed, the girl who was the subject of the alleged assault later made it clear that nothing happened reported the *Mail On Sunday*.

Kemal was found guilty of misusing her position, inappropriate behaviour (shouting) and failure to conduct herself appropriately; she was given a final warning because the most serious charge against her – of physical and verbal aggression – was 'unproven'.

She was allowed back to work, but not in Child Protection. Fearing further actions against her, she entered a claim for discrimination at an employment tribunal, which in early 2008 found in her favour by default, after Haringey failed to appear. Later, the council challenged that decision. A year later, the case was settled out of court.

Kemal said: 'I said to Sharon Shoesmith, "You can take everything from me: my home, my job, my good name, but you cannot strip me of my integrity. I'm not going to shut up. You don't know what is going on in Social Services, what is being concealed from you."

'I am sure she was misled by her managers. They are the ones that have to go. When Baby P died, I felt ashamed of us all. I feel ashamed of social work managers and ordinary social workers, and I feel in all this the real issue is being lost, that this little boy is rotting in a grave somewhere. How many "if only" are we going to go through, how many inquiries? Someone, somewhere, collectively has to take responsibility.'

In response Haringey Council issued a statement: 'Nevres Kemal was employed as a Senior Social Work Practitioner in the Referral and Assessment Team in August 2004. In October 2004 she raised concerns about a particular case. The matter was investigated. No breach of the statutory child protection procedures occurred and children were not at risk.

'The Commission for Social Care inspection has confirmed in a statement today that it was satisfied that the council had dealt properly with the individual case raised by Ms Kemal.

'Ms Kemal was subsequently suspended over a separate matter following an external complaint. She was dismissed in March 2007, caused by a breakdown of trust and confidence based on a substantial number of employment-related disputes over the course of her employment.

'An employment tribunal last year was settled without a hearing, with no admission of liability by the council. Nevres Kemal did not win her case in the ET [employment tribunal] nor did any tribunal make any findings concerning alleged whistleblowing.'

She was quoted in another paper as saying: 'I used to walk in after lunch and there would be piles of cases on my desk. Whatever cases came up when you were on duty would be yours – there would be 10 or 20. Because we were short, there were a lot of people working from agencies earning over £1,000-a-week but there was an attitude of "I don't care".'

Eventually Kemal was taken in to see Sharon Shoesmith: 'I told Sharon Shoesmith what was happening, but she said, "You don't know what's going on." I said, "It will be on your head. You will have blood on your hands, Sharon. You really don't run things here." She smiled and said, "Thank you." It got to the point where they sacked me.'

Indeed, this prompted Children's Secretary Ed Balls to state that the Government had followed the proper course of action in dealing with the whistleblower's information and had passed the matter on to the Commission for Social Care Inspection. A review by education watchdog Ofsted and the CSCI highlighted a number of 'issues for improvement' at Haringey and ordered the council to resolve them 'as soon as possible'. Social workers were told to raise their game.

Mr Balls remarked: 'It was clear that the correct procedures said this should be given to the inspector who has the responsibility to act. They have acted by having a meeting with Haringey and they were satisfied in this case. Things were done properly then but there is a wider issue which is raised by the serious case review, which is whether Haringey have acted properly in the case of Baby P. That is being investigated now. I will wait for the report, but I will then do what it takes so that, while we can't take away the pain and suffering of this poor little boy, we can take the action required to ensure not just accountability, but also that we prevent this happening in the future.'

Michael Gove said: 'The public are tired of hearing that "correct procedures have been followed" when a child died in agony. Ministers were told six months before Baby P's death there were profound problems in Haringey's children's department. Yet all that appears to have happened is the sacking and gagging of the whistleblower and bureaucratic buck-passing in Whitehall.'

The CSCI's response was: 'We raised these issues directly with Haringey at a formal meeting on March 12, 2007 and were satisfied that the council had dealt properly with the individual case raised by Ms Kemal.'

David Cameron remarked: 'This is an absolutely tragic case of a baby who seems to have fallen through the cracks of a bureaucratic system. If letters are sent with both Haringey and children in the same sentence, that should have been a real wake-up call.

'It seems bureaucratic changes in how inspections are carried out didn't help. It seems everyone is saying procedures were followed rather than asking who was responsible and why didn't they act.'

Meanwhile, the CSCI insisted: 'We raised these issues directly with Haringey at a formal meeting on March 12, 2007 and were satisfied that the council had dealt properly with the individual case raised by Ms Kemal.'

The importance of Nevres Kemal's allegations, even though she was not involved in the Baby P case, are that they get to the heart of the circumstances surrounding his death: a systemic failure that needed to be addressed and corrected to prevent further tragedies occurring. Or, as one newspaper put it – 'Haringey Council is a Basket Case.'

8

MORE HORRORS
EMERGE

B Y NOW the Baby P scandal dominated newspaper
headlines and television bulletins. The behaviour of those
involved, not just the perpetrators of the horror, but the ones
who should have helped him, was under the microscope.

New characters in the story emerged daily and a BBC
Panorama programme was to make fresh allegations about the
handling of the case when it reported that a senior manager at
Haringey Social Services, Clive Preece, overruled the concerns of
colleagues and senior police officers to return Baby P to his
mother. The programme said that social worker Sylvia Henry
had decided in December 2006, after Peter was taken to hospital
with non-accidental injuries, that he should be taken into foster
care, only to be overruled. She had arranged a placement for him
but it was decided after discussions with senior managers that
the toddler should instead be looked after by a family friend.

In her witness statement, given to police and seen by the
programme, Ms Henry said that she was 'very reluctant' to
allow the child to go to the family friend, Angela Godfrey, but

was bound by the Children Act 1989 to explore options fully with extended family and friends.

In her statement, she said: 'My impression of Angela was that she believed the local authority was overreacting and that the explanation for Baby P's injuries were those of his mother's, that they were caused by rough play and by his head-banging.'

Worried about Peter's wellbeing, Ms Henry delayed his return to his mother, agreeing with police that the child should remain out of her care. According to the programme, 'What Happened to Baby P?', she was told by a more senior colleague, Clive Preece, that he should be allowed home.

Ms Henry said that she had kept the foster place open, but because there was no evidence for a prosecution, 'reluctantly it was agreed that with changes to the home environment in place and all the support services in place with the family, there were little grounds for Baby P to remain out of the care of his mother.'

Miss Henry, a team manager at the Tottenham Social Services office, was 'very reluctant' to allow him to be given to Miss Godfrey and that was why she had arranged foster care.

When Mr Preece told Miss Henry that Baby P should go home, she claimed that she tried to delay because the police also believed that Baby P should remain 'out of the care of his mother.' But because the mother was not going to be prosecuted for cruelty, Miss Henry said there was nothing she could do.

Panorama also reported a clash between police and Social Services over the care of Baby P when his mother was arrested for a second time on suspicion of child cruelty in June 2007 and a police report said there was 'a frank exchange of views.' But the police relented and Baby P was returned home for the final time.

Haringey issued a series of denials over the programme and claims that its officials overruled police and social worker concerns to return Baby P to his mother. A spokesman said Mr Preece did not overrule concerns and insisted: 'No concerns were raised regarding placement with the friend at the time of the placement.' In a statement, the council said the decision to return Baby P to his mother in January 2007 was made by 'a multi-agency meeting' and agreed by police.

In relation to the claims of disagreements with the police, it said that a 'rigorous discussion' between professionals was to be expected when dealing with Child Protection and that the police agreed to the final plans for Baby P. However, the council insisted: 'The outcome of the discussion referred to was that the police agreed with the way forward. We wanted the police investigation to proceed as quickly as possible.'

The council maintained the police had never expressed the view, quoted in the programme, that Children's Services were too 'parent-focused'. Specifically, Haringey also denied that Mr Preece had overruled social workers, while maintaining 'no concerns' had been raised about the original plan to place the baby with Ms Godfrey at the time of the placement. Although the police report quoted contained criticism of social workers for being too optimistic about Baby P's mother and not focused sufficiently on the child, Haringey said such views were not expressed at the time and some had been formed, 'with the benefit of hindsight.'

The police were also involved in the probe into what went wrong at that December meeting when they and social workers were alerted to the fact that Tracey Connelly was seeing a new man but failed to investigate his background, the programme said.

Had police pursued this further, background checks would have revealed that he had been prosecuted by the RSPCA for cruelty to animals and that he was suspected of torturing his own grandmother to make her change her will in his favour.

A leaked police report concerning the December 2006 meeting said the information was 'not expanded' and police have always insisted they did not know a man was living at the house.

If Sharon Shoesmith so notably failed to apologise over the case, at least the Leader of Haringey Council George Meehan apologised fully on 18 November for the failure of its Child Protection agencies to save the life of Baby P. Before a scheduled meeting of the council, he said (and it is only right that this should be reproduced in full): 'I want, as Leader of the Council, to make this formal apology on behalf of Haringey Council at this first meeting of the cabinet. I will do so again to the meeting of the full council next week. These are the right places for Haringey to formally acknowledge our deep sorrow for these tragic events. Let me begin by making clear that we are very sorry for the events which led up to the death of Baby P, sorry for the suffering he endured, sorry for the failure of all the Child Protection agencies involved to protect him to save his life.

'Haringey Council's apology is heartfelt and unreserved.

'It is made to all those who knew and cared for the wellbeing of Baby P, it is made to all those residents of Haringey who feel let down by the actions of the Child Protection agencies in our area and concerned for the future of every other child at risk, and it is made to the wider public who will have listened with horror at the dreadful damage done during the tragically short life of Baby P.

'We are truly sorry. We await the outcome of the review, we will not comment in detail on the case until then, we will take whatever action is necessary to improve the protection of vulnerable children in Haringey.

'Let me conclude by saying this: in the 15 months since Baby P died, Haringey's social workers have continued to do their best, often in very difficult circumstances, to protect vulnerable children in our community. Despite the pressure of the last few months and weeks, they continue to put the interests of those children first. Whilst it is right for the review to identify faults and failures, it is important, in all the millions of words reported on the Baby P case, to recognise that denigrating their service does nothing to improve Child Protection.

'Colleagues, there is no failure to apologise in full by this council – we do so unreservedly tonight as we did last week. There is no failure to recognise our accountability – we do so and await the report of the review.

'There has, however, been failure: by all the agencies involved to protect this little child from the pain and suffering which led to his death, and for that we are truly and genuinely sorry.'

For days there had been a stream of reports on an Ed Balls' 'hit team' heading for Haringey. Robert Gorrie, the Lib Dem opposition leader, called it a 'disgrace' and called on Mr Meehan to resign.

At the same time as Meehan's apology the seemingly impossible happened: yet more details of chances to save poor Peter emerged. By now, one might have thought there could have been no more occasions to hand him a lifeline, but this wouldn't prove to be the case.

It emerged that a police probe into Connelly was dropped despite warnings from three doctors that his injuries could have been caused by abuse. The doctors said that his bruises were 'suggestive of non-accidental injury', but the Crown Prosecution Service (CPS) decided there was insufficient evidence to bring the case to trial.

Connelly had been arrested twice on suspicion of assaulting him, but gave a string of implausible and contradictory excuses to social workers, police and health officials.

Scotland Yard's child abuse unit compiled a file on the case, which included the statements from the doctors. This was then handed to the CPS, but lawyers there said they could not prove how and when the injuries were caused, or who had inflicted them. The CPS told police to drop the assault investigation and Connelly was told, on 2 August 2007, that no further action would be taken. A day later, Peter was dead.

The doctors' warnings raise questions about Haringey council's repeated decisions to send the toddler back to the home where he died.

Police said they did not want the child returned to his mother while they were investigating her for assault and frontline social worker Sylvia Henry, as described, urged her managers to place him with a foster family.

A newspaper report quoted a CPS spokesman refusing to confirm that the doctors who raised the alarm were consultant paediatricians Heather Mackinnon and Metta Jorgensson and family GP, Jerome Ikwueke. However, the trio all gave evidence to the Old Bailey trial that they were deeply concerned about Baby P's injuries. He was first taken to Dr Ikwueke on 1 December 2006, with bruises to his forehead, chest and shoulder, and the GP instructed his mother to take him to hospital. He told the trial that Tracey Connelly was 'flustered and agitated' and tried to blame the bruises on the boy's grandmother: 'I couldn't get a history of how it happened. She said it was the fault of the grandmother. I was not satisfied with the explanation.' Concerned, he contacted a junior doctor at the Whittington Hospital in north London and Baby P was seen by Dr Jorgensson, who discovered a 2in swelling on his forehead, bruises on his cheek and arm, and scratches to his right leg and shoulder. She was also 'alarmed' to find that Baby P had extensive bruising on both buttocks.

Dr Jorgensson said the mother 'seemed surprised' by the injuries and gave no immediate explanation for them, but within minutes she said her dogs – a German Shepherd and a Staffordshire bull terrier – could have jumped on him.

The next day Baby P was admitted to the hospital where he was this time examined by Dr Mackinnon. Connelly told Dr Mackinnon that the bruises might be from 'climbing on the sofa and falling on his bottom.' She even tried to claim one bruise had been caused by Dr Ikwueke.

After examining the child, Dr Mackinnon called Social Services and police. Under caution, the mother was interviewed by child protection officer Angela Slade later that day and gave yet another explanation. DC Slade informed the jury: 'She told me that her son was a lively child and he had a habit of banging his head on the cot bars.'

Connelly was arrested on suspicion of assault on 19

December, but protested her innocence and three days later DC Slade was at the social services meeting when Baby P was put on Haringey's Child Protection Register.

Detectives advised that Baby P should not be returned to his mother and social services managers placed him with a family friend for five weeks, but he was then handed back to her. In April 2007, Baby P was admitted to North Middlesex Hospital with bruises to his face. However, the police – who were still investigating the assault allegations – were not even told about the incident.

Another doctor, perhaps the most high-profile involved, also spoke for the first time about Peter. Dr Sabah Al-Zayyat, criticised for failing to spot his broken ribs and back during an examination just days before he died, talked of the 'shocking and tragic circumstances of his death.' The doctor, who was facing an investigation and had been banned from working unsupervised, said in a statement that she had been 'deeply affected' by events.

Dr Al-Zayyat, who qualified in Pakistan and worked in Saudi Arabia before coming to Britain in 2004, was, of course, the one who examined Baby P at a child development clinic at St Ann's Hospital shortly before his death. She noticed bruises to his body, but, as we have heard, decided she could not carry out a full systemic examination as the boy was 'miserable and cranky'. The post-mortem examination later revealed injuries, including a broken back and ribs, believed to have been obtained prior to the examination.

Dr Al-Zayyat subsequently had her contract with Great Ormond Street Hospital, which is responsible for Child Services in Haringey, terminated and in a statement made through the

Medical Protection Society, which gives professional indemnity to healthcare professionals, she said: 'Like everyone involved in this case, I have been deeply affected by the shocking and tragic circumstances of this young child's death. My professional career has been devoted to the care of children. I will co-operate with any investigation to identify whether lessons can be learnt from this case.'

A week later she was banned from practising when the General Medical Council suspended her registration.

While statements were being issued here and reports compiled there, in a quiet part of London, not far from the North Circular Road, an impromptu shrine to Peter was growing by the day.

Remembrance Garden, next to St Pancras and Islington Crematorium, East Finchley, became the focus for public outrage about the case. There, countless flowers and wreaths were placed by people who had never known Peter – mountains of letters, poems, soft toys and bouquets of roses, lilies and carnations.

One mourner said: 'I don't want to leave, to be quite honest. As a mum, like every mum across the country, we're all feeling it. I'm just absolutely devastated, I'm heartbroken.'

Details also emerged of how Peter's natural father had played a pivotal role in arranging a touching farewell for a group of family and friends in November of the previous year. One still-grieving relative said: 'We've spent days hearing how nobody gave a damn for Baby P – but it's not true. The family were told not to say anything because of the court case and it has been very difficult for all of us, particularly the little lad's father.

115

'The fact is, lots of people loved him very much. They just weren't aware of what was happening to him.'

The relative added: 'Baby P was in a tiny white coffin, which was taken to the crematorium chapel in the back of a hearse. There were four black funeral cars and a whole motorcade of private vehicles. People had travelled from all over the country because he came from a big, extended family. There were dozens of floral tributes, including some in the shape of teddies and one with a card bearing the words, "Little Man".

'The coffin was carried into church by his dad and his uncles. It was a terribly emotional sight. It was bright sunshine and birds were singing. It was like the heavens were smiling down on him.

'Baby P's dad addressed the mourners, which was very brave of him. He told everyone to remember all the happy times they had with his son and not dwell on the awful fate that befell him. He was in tears – everyone was – but he kept himself together somehow.'

The music Baby P's father chose for the occasion included the hymn, 'The Lord Is My Shepherd' and Eric Clapton's heart-rending 'Tears In Heaven'. Rocker Eric wrote the song after his own son Conor, 4, fell to his death from a 53rd-floor apartment window in New York in 1991.

The relative said: 'As the mourners filed out, they played Nat King Cole's "Smile". Everybody was overcome and sobbing. Baby P's mother was banned, but members of her family were there. They were made most welcome by the father's family.'

Baby P's ashes were scattered near the spot where those of his grandmother and grandfather were laid.

A newspaper later arranged for a granite plaque to be placed at the scene and two weeks after the end of the trial, 1,000 mourners – members of the public – turned up at the cemetery to remember him. They arrived before dawn and some were still coming through the gates as snow and rain fell in the darkness.

A petition for justice for Baby P by the country's largest-selling daily newspaper, the *Sun*, had over a million signatures on-line and in the post. It was the largest campaign in any newspaper history and backed its demands for action to be taken against the key people it said had failed to help the child. The petitions were eventually delivered to Downing Street by the sack-load.

They urged Beverley Hughes and Ed Balls to ensure Sharon Shoesmith, Haringey's head of Children's Services, Gillie Christou, head of the Child Protection Register, social workers Maria Ward and Sylvia Henry and Dr Sabah Al-Zayyat lose their jobs.

As the furore continued, news was also released that sadly showed that although Baby P's death was truly tragic and the case was appalling, it was far from being alone in shaming the nation.

Ofsted revealed that on average 4 children die every week in England in a system that offers 'patently inadequate' standards of care in the networks of schools, care workers and children's homes established to protect them. Councils had systematically failed to learn from the mistakes made in dozens of the most serious cases of child abuse, while too many frontline staff in schools and health centres are still unable to recognise signs of abuse.

In the first report from Ofsted since it took responsibility in

April 2007 for inspecting Child Protection facilities and assessing procedures, the watchdog raised urgent concerns about the system of serious case reviews, which are launched in the worst cases of abuse to help councils learn from mistakes made in their Child Protection teams.

Between April 2007 and August 2008, local authorities reported 424 serious incidents, including 282 child deaths, 136 cases of serious harm and 6 in which the outcome was unknown. One in four cases involved babies of under 12 months. Of 92 serious case reviews, 38 were rated inadequate and 34 just satisfactory – a rating Ofsted understandably said was not good enough.

This led to serious delays in judging what went wrong in the Child Protection system in 'almost all' of the cases, the report said. In one frightening, unnamed example, it took a local authority four years to conduct a single serious case review, during which time other children could have come to harm. The report warned that some instances of serious abuse were going unreported by local authorities. One in four did not report a single case for review.

Christine Gilbert, Ofsted's chief inspector, welcomed some improvements but admitted that she was frustrated that too many services were 'patently inadequate' and improvement was 'unacceptably slow'. 'Too many vulnerable children are still being let down by the system and we are failing to learn from the worst cases of abuse,' she said.

Referring to the Baby P case, she said: 'I wish I could guarantee that such a case would never happen again. I can't give that guarantee. Everyone working in Child Protection has to stop, take stock and look at what they are doing.'

Symptoms of abuse were being missed by frontline staff such as teachers and health workers, still too ready to 'accept at face value' any injuries which could be signs of abuse. Procedures designed to ensure staff working with children talk to each other – a recommendation after the death of Victoria Climbie – were poor in many areas: 'Consequently, necessary actions may not be taken to reduce the risks to children of sexual exploitation and drug or alcohol misuse.'

Beverley Hughes, the children's minister, commented: 'I am very concerned that the report says that staff in some services are not equipped to recognise and respond to signs of abuse and neglect. Everybody working with children has a clear duty to keep them safe. There are no excuses for ignorance.'

Although at this stage both Tracey Connelly and Steven Barker's identities had not been made known through the courts, millions already knew. Vigilantes had launched an internet poster campaign, creating fears that the friends and families of those responsible for the toddler's death might face revenge attacks.

Their faces were unveiled alongside Jason Owen, 36, in the e-posters sent to a wide range of organisations and individuals, including Kenny MacAskill, 50, justice secretary in the Scottish Parliament. The e-mail fliers include a vivid description of the tragic tot's injuries: 'These are the faces of the people who killed little Baby P. These people are being protected by the courts for the disgusting crime that they committed. Even if the courts convict me for showing the sick bastards, at least I took steps to show the world. Remember their faces – why protect these animals?' Copies of other posters also started to appear near

Penshurst Road showing Connelly's face along with the words 'vile woman' and named all three culprits, before adding: 'They deserve to die!' The woman's friends were also named.

The identities of the 27-year-old mother and her 32-year-old boyfriend were taken down from the British Army Rumour Service website moments after being posted. But the images were on social networking site Facebook too and the couple's names were also available as an answer to a query on a popular search engine 15 hours after being posted.

It was the latest stage in a sustained hate campaign against the couple and Owen, calling for violent retribution.

The previous week Facebook had shut down pages carrying threats and abusive comments about the mother, including one entitled: 'Death is too good for Tracey Connelly, torture the bitch that killed Baby P.'

The mother's profile page on Bebo was subsequently removed after abusive messages had been added by those who were confident that they could breach existing court injunctions without being traced.

We have already learned earlier in this book about life in Penshurst Road and the almost unbearable treatment handed out to Peter, yet still more grizzly details were to emerge.

One of the witnesses to the brutality was Jason Owen's 15-year-old lover, who had given key video evidence at the trial. As Ed Balls was about to reveal the results of the report into the affair, she spoke in even greater detail of the nightmare existence there, 24 hours a day.

The conditions there have already been discussed, but the girl's further description of the house – where even Barker's pet

Rottweiler would shake in fear when his owner came near – makes compelling reading.

The girl's own description, given in a newspaper interview, makes it seem all the more inexplicable that Peter was allowed to stay there by the authorities. For example, when Connelly told Barker she might be pregnant, he threatened to 'butcher' her: 'I heard it all. He smashed the bedroom door in and said he was going to cut her up if she was pregnant. He was furious. She was screaming and crying, and he was going mad.'

Connelly left her children at the mercy of Barker, never feeding or changing the youngest ones: 'And I never saw her cuddle or kiss them either. They'd just play by themselves. And all the kids had lice, it was nasty. You could see them on their eyebrows. She wasn't a mum at all. She must have known what was going on with her baby. She never said, "What are these bruises on my baby?" But she'd lie and tell me Baby P had hurt himself tripping over his toys.'

The only time she ever saw Connelly show Baby P any affection was at her own birthday party – and only because her pals were there: 'She was a bit tipsy and dancing with Peter, holding his hands and cooing at him,' the girl told the *News of the World*. 'I don't think he knew what was going on. He seemed surprised. She didn't normally pay him any attention but because her friends were there, she was showing an interest.'

Although Barker was cruel to the children, he was different with Connelly: 'They were always cuddling and kissing. There'd be lots of loud noises coming from their bedroom. They were all over each other the whole time – she was a sex maniac.

'The kids seemed used to it.'

So desperate were the men in the house to escape notice of them living there in case it affected Connelly's weekly £400-plus benefits that the girl and Barker had to spend an hour in a nearby cemetery when a social worker called, in order not to be spotted.

Before leaving, Barker had tried to hide the marks of his violence on Peter's face by smearing him with chocolate from a pack of digestive biscuits: 'It seemed like a routine thing for him. When we got back, the mum was laughing and joking. It was like she'd got away with it.

'I wanted to tell somebody. They should have known what was going on from the way Baby P looked. I was amazed they'd been fooled by a bit of chocolate. If only they'd wiped his face.' And the girl – one of eight youngsters in the home – also expressed what many others were subsequently amazed about.

'It should have been obvious to the social worker that more people were living in the house. There were shoes and coats and lots of toothbrushes in the bathroom. There was even Steven's weight-training machine in the dining room.

'Peter would look at Steven and I could see how he was terrified. He didn't laugh very much, he wasn't happy or smiley – that poor baby didn't have a chance.

'He was a beautiful baby with lovely blond hair. I have a relative about the same age who laughs and giggles the whole time, but Baby P was not like that. He was so different – quiet, very scared. And his mum must have picked up on that.

'I was really scared because of what I'd seen – I thought he'd do that to me, his eyes were evil. When he was hurting Peter, he'd look at me and grin. He was evil all the time. There was no fun and laughter in the house. He made my skin crawl and made me feel physically sick.'

As well as Connelly's children, there were three of Jason's in the house too, the eldest just a year younger than the girlfriend herself: 'We were told we weren't to pick the baby up. His mother was the only one allowed to do it. The baby's room was at the top of the stairs and I wasn't allowed in.

'He used to be in there by himself quite often, during the day as well the night. He'd call out for his "Mum-my" – that's how he'd say it – but she never went to him. It's heartbreaking. It was the only word I knew he could say. He'd cry for a little bit and realise no one was coming.

'Baby P was lovely. He had curly blond hair, but they shaved it off. I think it was because of those scabs on his head. It made him look even sadder.

'He wouldn't come to adults. He wouldn't even look around when he played with his toys; he'd focus on one spot as if he didn't want people to see him and play with his teddies quietly to avoid attention.'

She says all eight children in the house, including her, knew better than to make any noise when Barker, the stepfather, was around – they had to do as he told them. If he instructed them to collect their clothes together and wasn't satisfied with the way they did it, he would grab the clothes off them and throw them around the room to make them start all over again.

Barker spent a lot of his time glued to television programmes about Hitler and, just to amuse himself, he would train Peter to give a Nazi salute.

'About two weeks after I moved in, I started to see something wasn't right about the way the stepfather was with the kids,' the girl revealed. 'The first thing I seen was when he told Baby P and his sister to climb up and down on the sofa. They did it until they were really crying. He must have been getting a kick out of it somehow. He was finding it funny, he was smirking.'

Barker would often say how he didn't like coloured people and when he 'trained' Peter, he would click his fingers so the boy lowered his hand, just as if he were training a dog.

And she was also in the house on the day when they all realised that Peter's torment was finally over. The girl recalled one of the other youngsters screaming that Peter was dead, minutes after Barker went into the bedroom. While most of the household erupted into panic, Peter's mother seemed more concerned with herself – doing her hair and dressing before an ambulance was called. Meanwhile, Jason Owen tried to do mouth-to-mouth resuscitation on Peter's little body on the floor of his bedroom. The girl recalled: 'I could just see Jason hunched over; he was crying, but Steven just stood there. He didn't seem upset; he didn't care.

'I thought it was strange that Peter hadn't woken up earlier. It seemed quite late when his step-dad went into the room. I took the kids away from it all; we went down to the cemetery.'

After a while the brothers came out to meet the rest of the household and initially, Barker seemed quite calm. But then he must have realised that this would not be just another instance where he could fool Social Services quite so easily and so he persuaded his brother and the girl to run away with him.

Later, at the Epping campsite where they had fled to escape

police – while reading newspaper stories about Baby P's death – he confessed what he had done.

'He didn't even want to give his name when we arrived at the campsite,' the girl said. 'He was worried police would track him down. He got really angry and said that he did do it but that it wasn't his fault that he did it. And he said there was no way he was getting the blame for it. Later, when he calmed down, he denied he did anything. And he said he'd take us down with him if he was in trouble.

'When the case finally got to the Old Bailey and I was to give evidence, I wanted to go in the court and face him, to finally prove I wasn't scared of him any more. But in the end, the only way I could do it was by video-link.'

How much of that gruelling newspaper account the staff at Haringey Council read that last weekend in November is impossible to say. Doubtless, they would have on their minds the shattering report that Ed Balls was about to release to the world. Already, the leaks from Westminster had indicated that the report would be devastating in its tone. And so it was.

9

THE REPORT

ONE HEADLINE called it, THE DAY OF RECKONING. The *Sun* urged, GO NOW. Even the usually sedate *Times* predicted: COUNCIL BRACED FOR REMOVAL OF SENIOR MANAGERS. They all got it right, and then some. The day was 1 December 2008, and by the end of it, there wasn't just blood on the walls of Haringey Council, it was splattered on the ceiling, soaking into the keyboards and pouring through the banisters as well.

And the cause of all the bloodshed was the slim report – a mere 16 pages that the inspectors ordered by children's minister Ed Balls had delivered on Haringey Council. Upon examination, the seven-strong inspection team found failings in almost every area of the council's Child Protection Services. Virtually every page contained words such as 'inadequate', 'unacceptable', 'poor' and 'unreliable'.

Mr Balls himself described the report as 'devastating' and 'damning', and noted that it found, 'deep-rooted and fundamental failings' at the council.

The inspectors from Ofsted, the Healthcare Commission and

the Chief Inspector of Constabulary carried out the review in just 13 days. While that doesn't sound a great length of time, it was enough to discover a catalogue of 'serious concerns' about the safeguarding of children in Haringey.

Below are just some of the main faults they uncovered:

- Insufficient oversight of Child Protection Services by Haringey's councillors and senior officers
- Social workers, health professionals and police not communicating routinely and consistently
- A failure to identify children at immediate risk of harm
- Frontline procedures of inconsistent quality
- Generally poor Child Protection plans
- Record-keeping for case files were inconsistent and often poor
- An over-reliance on not always accurate performance data
- A failure to speak directly to children at risk
- Concerns that youngsters suspected of being abused may not have been able to speak up without fear
- The Serious Case Review into Baby P's death was inadequate
- A high turnover of social workers at Haringey Council had resulted in heavy reliance on agency staff, leading to a lack of continuity for children and their families
- Heavy workloads for social workers, with the true number of children allocated to them not always accurately counted
- A managerial failure to ensure all the requirements of the Inquiry into Victoria Climbie's murder in 2000 were met.

The report stated: 'The contribution of local services to improving outcomes for children and young people at risk or requiring safeguarding is inadequate and needs urgent and sustained attention.' It was officialese, but in plain English it meant that the council just wasn't up to the job of looking after children at risk, such as Baby P, and action needed to be quickly taken.

And it didn't take long for the first axe to fall: Sharon Shoesmith was stripped of her role as children's director, albeit still on full salary. Under the 1996 Education Act, Ed Balls used legal powers to move directly: 'I have powers to intervene and remove someone who is not fit for office. Most people would look at this report – look at the clear evidence of management failures – and say that this kind of failure should not be rewarded with compensation or payoffs. That's a matter for Haringey.' Although he had the power to remove Shoesmith from office, her employment was a matter for Haringey to resolve. Later, she said that the first heard of her axing was when she saw Mr Balls announce it on television.

In a formal statement, the council said: 'She has been suspended pending disciplinary proceedings, with two others – Cecilia Hitchen, deputy director, Children and Families and Clive Preece, head of Children in Need and Safeguarding Services.' Three other staff – social worker Maria Ward, senior social worker Sylvia Henry and team manager Gillie Christou were removed from Child Protection duties pending further investigation. Although she was suspended, the enquiry into Sylvia Henry's role eventually concluded that there was 'no case to answer'.

The Labour Council Leader George Meehan and Cabinet Member for Children, Liz Santry – who had been under constant pressure to resign – both quit after meeting Balls. The minister acted swiftly after he received the new inspectors' report into the failings from front-line to management, which also found that hospitals, police and even inspectors themselves all failed to review properly the death of Baby P.

Mr Balls refused to grant a new public inquiry into the case, claiming that he wanted 'to act now' rather than wait for a lengthy new investigation, but he did announce that every council would now have to learn the lessons of the tragedy and from then on, all NHS trusts would be asked to review their Child Protection policies.

Under rarely used powers, Mr Balls directed the council to remove Ms Shoesmith from power and install John Coughlan, in her place. In the wake of the Baby P trial, he had been seconded the previous month to oversee Children's Services. A new chair of the council's Safeguarding Board – which was meant to scrutinise its staff – was also appointed: Graham Badman would start work on a brand new 'serious case review' of the toddler's case the following week.

Mr Balls stressed that one of the most worrying findings of the report was that children were still being put at risk in Haringey. He said that the council failed to allow children suspected of being abused to give evidence on their own in private. It was crucial that these youngsters were, 'properly heard and able to speak up without fear.' He admitted that social workers were often 'unsung heroes', but stressed: 'They must also be accountable for the decisions and when things go badly wrong, people want to know why and what can be done about it.'

Mr Balls said that he would be 'astonished' if Shoesmith

received any compensation for losing her job. In fact, his remark was to be overtaken by events.

Council Robert Gorrie, Leader of the Lib-Dem opposition in the Haringey borough, remarked: 'The report is absolutely devastating.'

The previous month Shoesmith was the beneficiary of an open letter signed by 61 primary and secondary school head teachers in Haringey. Calling her an 'outstanding public servant', who had in her previous role revitalised Haringey's once shattered education service, it stated: 'Should the Child P case result in her loss from the borough, then our children and young people will lose one of their most effective, determined and committed champions.'

The new report, however, made it clear that the failings in the Baby P case were not just down to isolated mistakes by those on the front line, but staff at the highest level of management too. Shoesmith was therefore held accountable for what Ed Balls described as 'serious failings in practice and management' in Haringey's Children's Services department. The report prepared for Balls presented a 'damning verdict' on safeguarding children in Haringey, he said. Shoesmith had chaired the serious case review into the death of Baby P and Balls made it clear that this was 'inadequate', that it lacked true rigour.

Mr Balls admitted that he was particularly worried by a finding of the inspectors that Child Protection staff failed to talk directly to children: 'Where children were not seen alone, it worries me greatly that the inspectors found little evidence of management follow-up to ensure children suspected of being abused were properly heard and able to speak up without fear.'

He urged investigations into 38 other abuse cases to be reopened after Ofsted criticised the quality of previous reviews. They include three cases in Cornwall, three in Northamptonshire and deaths and serious injuries to children in Bristol, Derbyshire and Hampshire. Ofsted would also carry out annual, unannounced inspections in England.

There would be a fresh independent review of the Baby P case, with an executive summary published in March 2009, but the full report would remain confidential and Balls refused to order a full Public Inquiry. He accepted advice from Lord Laming, head of the Inquiry into the death of Victoria Climbie in 2000, who recommended that a Public Inquiry would set back progress on Child Protection made in many parts of England and divert effort from the actions needed to keep children safe in Haringey.

Mr Balls said that he was acting in response to overwhelming public anger that none of the officials charged with protecting Baby P had stepped in to halt his daily abuse. He described the inspectors' findings as 'devastating' and said that they showed the borough needed a new management team to ensure vulnerable children were properly protected: 'It's hugely disappointing and people are angry that when there was clear evidence of abuse in the case of Baby P, action did not occur and intervention did not happen quickly enough.'

The team of inspectors had not been required to review the Baby P case, but to look at the measures currently in place to protect other vulnerable children. They found failings in virtually every area of the council's Child Protection services.

George Meehan said that he was resigning for 'personal honour and local accountability.' In a statement, he admitted: 'We strived at every step to make the improvements necessary to prevent the kind of harm that was inflicted on Baby P by his guardians and we failed. As a mark of respect to Baby P and as a sign of the deep sorrow we feel, it is right and proper for me to resign the leadership of the council.'

As leader, Labour councillor Meehan, 65, had overall responsibility for Haringey's failures over Baby P. He had also been in power during the Victoria Climbie case.

Liz Santry, 63, also resigned. As cabinet member for children and young people was the councillor with direct responsibility for Child Protection.

Local Liberal Democrat MP Lynne Featherstone commented: 'I have never seen such a devastating critique of any authority as this report. Haringey is clearly and evidently beyond redemption.' She said that taxpayers in the borough would be 'disgusted' if Mrs Shoesmith were offered any payoff to leave.

Haringey's chief executive Dr Ita O'Donovan said the borough's heads of Legal Services and Human Resources would study Mrs Shoesmith's contract before making recommendations to a select committee of councillors, who would have to vote on any decision.

Liberal Democrat group leader Robert Gorrie remarked: 'There will be beyond doubt a massive degree of disdain on the streets of Haringey if there is not a dismissal or if taxpayers' money is used to compensate people who have failed in such a major way.'

Temporarily, Mrs Shoesmith was replaced by John Coughlan and Ed Balls said that he would appoint a permanent successor in January 2009.

Meanwhile, there was criticism from Michael Gove, who said the inspectors' review had shown that the Ofsted inspection regime had failed: 'A year ago, after Baby P had died, Ofsted said that Haringey provided a good service and now they paint a devastating picture of a dysfunctional council. The report also underlines how the current bureaucratic approach continues to fail to ensure clear accountability.'

Liberal Democrat children's spokesman David Laws said the investigations did not go far enough and called for a Public Inquiry: 'Ed Balls will hope that forcing resignations at Haringey Council will draw a line under this tragic case. However, if we are really to safeguard children in the future then we need more than just a few personnel changes at the top. Until the failings of this case are fully in, the Public Assessments fail to identify children at immediate risk of harm, or to act on that risk.'

The key players brought in were leading Social Services professionals John Coughlan and Graham Badman. Coughlan, 48, had been seconded from his £150,000-a-year post as Hampshire County Council's director of children's services to take over from the suspended Sharon Shoesmith. A former president of the Association of Directors of Children's Services, he was a respected local authority chief with more than 20 years' experience. A father-of-two, he studied English and History of Art at Leeds University before working in children's homes in Birmingham. Unlike Shoesmith, whose background was the education system, Coughlan had spent his entire career in Social Services.

The previous month, he had been brought in to work alongside Ms Shoesmith, but would be taking over the department until at least the following month. Among his first tasks would be to decide what action will be taken over the social workers named in the Baby P investigation.

In a statement, he said: 'The Secretary of State has asked me to address any immediate staffing issues raised in the Baby P case. Three social work staff are subject to review and will not be undertaking Child Protection duties pending further investigation. I will look as a matter of urgency at whether any further action is needed in the case of these individuals or any other staff. My first priority is to ensure the safety of children and young people in Haringey.'

Coughlan, who was handpicked by Ed Balls, described the high numbers of young people in custody as a 'national disgrace' and called for a reduction in red tape to allow councils to operate without being encumbered by time-consuming bureaucracy.

Two weeks earlier, Graham Badman, the new chairman of Haringey's Local Safeguarding Children Board, retired as Kent County Council's director of Children's Services. In his seven years in the role, he had been credited with introducing a tough code of conduct to prevent child abuse. The former science teacher had more than 35 years' experience and was awarded a CBE for Services to Children.

He spoke about the Baby P case to a committee in November 2008 when he said that no system could guarantee the safety of all children: 'Do we have procedures I am confident about? Yes, we do. Do we have the resources that I would wish? No, we do not. That is because in any process of dispensing public money, there is a rationing and conflicting priorities that members have to balance.'

His appointment to the Safeguarding Children board, which was responsible for investigating failures in Social Services, would at least give the body some independence as Shoesmith had jointly held the post despite an apparent conflict of interest.

It seemed pretty drastic measures had been taken, but there were others who considered they had 'not gone far enough.' That was exactly the wording used in a *Sun* headline above a story that read:

Bosses finally took action against six council bunglers in the Baby P tragedy last night, but stopped short of firing them – and all are still on full pay.

Shamed Sharon Shoesmith was suspended after a report on the scandal was handed to Children's Secretary Ed Balls. Yet she continues to receive the £110,000 salary paid to her as head of children's services in Haringey, North London.

Her deputy and a senior social worker were also suspended on full pay. And three more social workers had their futures placed 'under review', again with no reduction in their taxpayer-funded salaries.

David Cameron echoed the sentiment when he wrote in an article in the *Sun* that, 'the sackings, suspensions, resignations were long overdue. Thank God the Government answered our call for the independent inquiry that was needed.'

But other big questions remain unanswered. Why should the serious case review, which told the full story of what went wrong, remain top secret? The public would have to wait months to see a summary of the report. As Cameron said, 'That is totally unacceptable. It reveals serious mistakes that led to Baby P's death. It is vital that other professionals learn from these mistakes. What have they got to hide? Why can't the public read the facts in full? What kind of culture puts safeguarding the system before children, protecting bureaucrats before our babies?'

And he added in a television interview: 'If they failed, then they failed and they shouldn't be kept on full pay. They shouldn't be rewarded for that failure.

'It's good that some of the people have been named and been suspended, but we still have a lot to do to get to the bottom of what really happened and to learn all the lessons.'

Children's rights campaigner Camila Batmanghelidjh echoed Cameron's sentiments when she too wrote: 'The fact three staff have lost their jobs at Haringey Council does not solve the real problem. I'm afraid there are other Baby Ps – many of them – suffering abuse today. We need a complete reassessment of the whole system. Current social work structures cannot cope with demand. Governments have got away with it because abused children behind closed doors cannot protest. We shouldn't celebrate these staff losing their jobs. We should save the celebrations for when the whole system is fit for purpose.'

There was growing anger over the fact that those axed were still on full pay.

Michael Gove wrote to Haringey Council demanding to know how long the suspended employees would remain on full pay. He also asked the local authority to make Ms Shoesmith's contract public so that tax payers could see on what basis she was still employed.

In a letter to council chief executive Dr O'Donovan, Mr Gove wrote: 'Sharon Shoesmith has been judged unfit to continue in her role by an independent inquiry and the Secretary of State. Despite this, she still continues to draw a salary in excess of £100,000. Taxpayers will want to know why. What is being done to resolve this situation as speedily as possible?'

Liberal Democrat children's spokesman David Laws believed Haringey should sack Ms Shoesmith as Mr Balls did not have the power to do so. He said: 'I think it is totally inappropriate that, given the report that was issued yesterday and her removal from her position, she should remain on full pay.'

Haringey Council conceded that Shoesmith's case would be resolved as quickly as possible, but refused to discuss details. A spokesman said: 'The director is currently suspended. It is both normal practice and a part of the employment contract that suspension is on full pay. Disciplinary hearings for chief officers are conducted by a panel of councillors. The process for consideration of the case to be answered is being conducted as quickly as possible.'

But the dust hadn't even settled on the report and Ed Balls' response to it when the head of Ofsted claimed Haringey Council misled its inspectors by 'hiding behind' false data and that other local authorities could also be manipulating its system of rating Child Protection services.

Christine Gilbert, who vowed to shake up inspections, acknowledged mistakes were made in the monitoring of Haringey Council, which received a 'good' rating just weeks after Baby P's death. In an interview with the *Guardian*, Ms Gilbert said she was 'concerned' that there might be other local authorities that similarly supplied incorrect data to demonstrate their Child Protection services were adequate.

According to the *Guardian*, the week's review of Haringey Council showed managers had said children were assessed promptly when their files showed their assessments were incomplete. Files also revealed that assessments were often carried out in the presence of a parent or guardian, when they could be the person harming the child.

Ms Gilbert said: 'I think if the grades that we gave last December gave a false assurance we have to take some responsibility for that. That's one of the reasons that I'm saying we're looking again at our proposal [to reform inspection]. We need to do all we can from our position, so I'm not washing my hands of it.'

Gilbert promised that Ofsted would overhaul inspections of Child Protection services in recognition that mistakes were made in the monitoring of Haringey Council. Ofsted's assessment of local authorities' children's services in 2008 consisted of a checklist of the information that managers had to provide to demonstrate, among other things, that they had adequate social workers and were assessing children promptly. Managers in Haringey misled Ofsted by providing inaccurate data, the chief inspector told the the *Guardian*.

Gilbert added that it wasn't until inspectors in the week's review began pulling children's files from the office shelves in the town hall that they realised the extent of the deceit. Asked if there were other authorities that could similarly have supplied incorrect data to the previous year's reviews, she said: 'I am concerned that we look at the way this is happening... we're looking at the review of Haringey we undertook to see if there are any lessons we can learn. I would say that I am concerned.' However, she said the processes were already under review before the Baby P verdict, adding: 'We are looking at everything fresh again after this.'

Gilbert continued: 'I think that if the grades that we gave last December gave a false assurance, we have to take some responsibility for that. That's one of the reasons that I'm saying we're looking again at our proposals [to reform inspections]. We need to do all we can from our position so I'm absolutely not washing my hands of it.'

Ofsted has been criticised after it emerged that the council was rated 'good' in a performance assessment, largely based on data provided by Haringey officials. Former head teacher Gilbert, who became education chief in Tower Hamlets, described the week's joint area review report into Baby P's death, the results of which were not being made public, as 'devastating'.

'By the second day the inspectors were saying the things they were finding were really inadequate, there seemed to be a catalogue of concerns,' she continued.

In September 2008, Ofsted announced proposals to overhaul the current inspection regime for safeguarding children. These included three-year rolling inspections of Children's Services in every area with spot checks to assess the risk in every area and prioritise who would receive the first batch of inspections.

'I think that the processes that we're proposing will be better than the processes that we had,' said Gilbert. Even so, she admitted that the new processes 'couldn't absolutely guarantee that there would not be a tragedy like this.'

Gilbert admitted that across the UK there were still serious failings on the part of separate agencies working with children to communicate with each other, despite the review following the death in Haringey of Victoria Climbie, which ordered a fundamental restructure of services to make them join up more so children would not slip through the net. However, she said that she hoped some good would come out of the situation. It was hard to see the positive side with something so tragic, she agreed, but, 'I think that every partnership in the country, every local authority, almost as we speak, is reviewing what it's doing, asking itself hard questions.'

She expressed fears that the high profile of the Baby P case would trigger a shortage of social workers: 'The real worry is about recruitment to social work [and] the damage done to the morale of social workers, most of whom do a hard job very well.'

By that weekend Ed Balls was saying that he wanted to 'transform' the role of social workers as the Government prepared to launch a root-and-branch overhaul of the profession in the wake of Baby P. Officials confirmed that Mr Balls and health secretary Alan Johnson were to announce the formation of a new task force to look at every aspect of social work in England, including leadership, training and recruitment.

Mr Balls acknowledged that the changes ministers were planning would be 'controversial', but said that he was determined to ensure that the professionals entrusted with child safety carried out their task properly. He said that social workers should be put on the same footing as the teaching profession, which has been 'transformed' over the past 10 years.

'The thing I want to do now is to do the same thing for social workers as we have done for teachers: to improve their training, to improve the quality of leadership, to improve the incentives for people who rise up through the system,' he told BBC1's *Politics Show*.

Officials said ministers wanted to see future chiefs of local authority Children's Services gain experience in schools and social work before they are appointed. Training schemes would be changed, with more emphasis on 'on-the-job' learning and the introduction of a new 'qualifying year' in which new staff would get hands-on experience before they were fully qualified. In addition, it was expected that better-performing social workers would be paid more to work in 'tough frontline areas'.

'In my view, the training of social workers is too theoretical. There isn't enough on-the-job training,' said Mr Balls. 'We need our schools and our social workers to work more closely together, we need to boost leadership; there's lots to be done.'

The Department for Children, Schools and Families (DCSF) said that the new taskforce would be headed by Moira Gibb, the chief executive of Camden Council and a former social worker, and would report to ministers by the following summer.

A DCSF spokeswoman said that it would be a 'nuts and bolts review' of social work practice. 'We know that we have not done enough to support excellence in social work,' she said. 'We have been working for a while on a workforce strategy.'

The announcement was welcomed by Sue Berelowitz, deputy children's commissioner for England. 'The introduction of a new qualifying year in which staff will get hands-on experience before they qualify is a particularly sensible improvement,' she said.

Michael Gove said real improvements could only be achieved by learning the lessons from previous tragedies: 'That means making public as much information as possible about what has gone wrong in the past, including publishing the Serious Case Review from Haringey, which currently remains secret.'

Liberal Democrat children's spokesman David Laws said: 'While any additional training for social workers is welcome, this does rather sound like closing the stable door after the horse has bolted.'

A week after the Ofsted report, the door was finally closed on Sharon Shoesmith. She was dismissed on 8 December 2008 with no payoff by a panel of three councillors with immediate effect, although she was reported to be retaining a pension pot of £1.5 million. They awarded her no compensation and no payment in lieu of her notice period. In a statement, the council said that she would not work for the local authority again.

Despite the report, she had not chosen to resign and Haringey Council took a week to go through its employment procedures.

MP Lynne Featherstone commented: 'I very much welcome her departure without a single penny. Hopefully it marks a break with the culture of secrecy, failure and deceit that failed Baby P. Under her watch, inspectors and the people of Haringey were lied to and those who sought to challenge her were silenced. Once the truth was finally uncovered, the horrific catalogue of failings clearly amount to wilful neglect of duty on her part.'

Robert Gorrie remarked: 'This is another step in the difficult journey of rebuilding confidence in our borough's Children's Services. Those in top jobs in public service should be put on notice – there is no hiding place for incompetence and deceit for those charged with looking after the vulnerable children in our society.'

Ed Balls' spokesperson said: 'Her employment was a matter for Haringey. The Secretary of State is satisfied they have moved swiftly to resolve this.'

A Haringey source was quoted as saying the review had 'highlighted inadequate management of arrangements for safeguarding children.' The source added: 'The content of the report led to a fundamental loss of trust and confidence in Ms Shoesmith.'

A statement from Haringey Council added: 'Sharon Shoesmith has been dismissed with immediate effect. Ms Shoesmith will not be returning to work in Haringey. She will not receive any compensation package. She will not receive any payment in lieu of notice.'

As Shoesmith's dismissal closed one chapter in the story of the aftermath of Baby P's death, it is worthwhile to examine in detail the reasoning behind it by reproducing the full statement made by Ed Balls during that fateful week. It makes devastating reading:

The whole nation has been shocked and moved by the tragic and horrific death of Baby P. All of us find it impossible to comprehend how adults could commit such terrible acts of evil against this little boy. And the public is angry that nobody stepped in to prevent this tragedy from happening.

I want to say very clearly at the outset: social workers, police officers, GPs, health professionals, all the people who work to keep children safe do a very difficult job, often in really challenging circumstances – all around the country and in particular in Haringey. They make difficult judgments every day that help to keep children safe – and many of them are unsung heroes. But they must also be accountable for their decisions. And where things go badly wrong, people are right to want to know why and what will be done about it.

In the case of Baby P, things did go tragically wrong. I received the full confidential Serious Case Review into the death of Baby P on the morning of 12 November. After studying it and seeing the clear failings of practice and management that it highlighted, I immediately arranged for the secondment to Haringey of John Coughlan, the Director of Children's Services in Hampshire, to oversee that proper procedures for safeguarding children are in place and being followed.

We also immediately decided that Ofsted, the Healthcare Commission and the Chief Inspector of Constabulary should carry out an urgent inspection of safeguarding in Haringey.

At 6 o'clock yesterday evening, I received the final draft of the inspectors' report. The Children's Minister and I studied it overnight with our experts. Her Majesty's Chief Inspector Christine Gilbert presented the final report to us at 9 o'clock this morning and to Haringey Council shortly thereafter. And copies of the final report and my response have been passed to the Home Secretary, the Health Secretary, the Opposition spokespeople, the two local MPs and the Chairman of the Select Committee.

This morning, I met with the Leader, Deputy Leader, Lead

Member for Children's Services and Chief Executive of Haringey Council to discuss the report's findings and my response. I am grateful for Haringey's co-operation and agreement to act upon my decisions. And as you will know, in the last hour, the Leader of the Council and the Lead Member for Children's Services have announced their resignations.

Over the past fortnight, as part of their work, the Inspectors have studied the case files on Baby P and his family, the full Serious Case Review and a significant number of other Child Protection case files – and their report delivers a damning verdict on the current management of safeguarding in Haringey.

In their summary judgment, the Inspectors say that there are a number of serious concerns in relation to safeguarding of children and young people in Haringey. The contribution of local services to improving outcomes for children and young people at risk or requiring safeguarding is inadequate and needs urgent and sustained attention.

They find that: the arrangements for the leadership and management of safeguarding by the local authority and partner agencies are inadequate.

The catalogue of failings reported to me – many of which are clearly apparent in the case of Baby P – include:

- A failure to identify those children and young people at immediate risk of harm and to act on evidence
- Agencies generally working in isolation from one another and without any effective co-ordination
- Poor gathering, recording and sharing of information

- Inconsistent quality of front-line practice and insufficient evidence of supervision by senior management
- Insufficient management oversight of the Assistant Director of Children's Services by the Director of Children's Services and Chief Executive
- Incomplete reporting of the management audit report by senior officials to elected members
- Insufficient challenge by the Local Safeguarding Children Board to its members and also to front-line staff
- An over dependence on performance data, which was not always accurate and poor Child Protection plans.

The Inspectors also highlight a failure to talk directly to children at risk and where children were not seen alone, it worries me greatly that the Inspectors find little evidence of management follow-up to ensure that children suspected of being abused were properly heard and able to speak up without fear. Furthermore, in the particular case of Baby P, Ofsted has judged the Serious Case Review into his death to be inadequate.

Having studied the nine individual agency management reports on which the Serious Case Review is based, the inspectors judged:

- Only three to be good.
- One to be adequate and five to be inadequate – with the reports from Haringey Children's Social Care Services and the Haringey Teaching Primary Care Trust judged to "lack rigour in their analysis and thus significantly undermine the integrity of the Serious Case Review."

And they conclude that as a result, the Serious Case Review misses important opportunities to ensure lessons are learned.

Overall, the Inspectors' findings are – I have to say – devastating. Their report sets out detailed recommendations, all of which must now be accepted in full. And having studied their report, I have decided to take immediate action.

My first priority is to put in place a new leadership and management team in Haringey Children's Services to ensure that vulnerable children in the borough are properly protected. I have directed Haringey Council to appoint John Coughlan as Director of Children's Services.

Haringey Council will now remove the current Director of Children's Services from her post with immediate effect.

Mr Coughlan is one of the most highly respected directors of children's services in the country and I am grateful that he has agreed to extend his secondment to Haringey to manage the transition to new management.

My direction takes place under section 497A (4B) of the Education Act 1996. It takes immediate effect and will last until 31 December 2008.

I will identify a new director of children's services to take up post from 1 January 2009 and it is my intention to direct this appointment too.

As a result of my direction, Mr Coughlan will now be in charge of making all appointments in Haringey Children's Services. He has decided that Libby Blake should be appointed as his deputy so I am also directing her appointment. Ms Blake is currently seconded to Haringey from Kensington and Chelsea, where she is director for family services.

I have asked Mr Coughlan to consider and address any immediate staffing issues raised by the Baby P case. Mr Coughlan will consider further staffing capability in Haringey Children's Services in the coming days. I am sure that he will have the full support of all Haringey staff as he prepares to implement the recommendations of the Inspectors' report.

'I have asked Mr Coughlan and his successor to provide me with monthly reports. I have also asked Ofsted to review the progress made on the implementation of the Inspectors' recommendations and report to me by the end of June.

On the basis of these regular reports and the report from Ofsted, I will then decide whether further sanction is needed – and in particular whether I should use my statutory powers to require the Council to enter into a contractual arrangement with an external provider for the delivery of some or all of its' Children's Services. And in the meantime, if I am not satisfied that there is sufficient progress, I will not hesitate to intervene again. But I believe that I need to go further now to ensure that all the Inspectors' findings are acted upon across all local agencies and that all the lessons of the Baby P case are learned and acted upon.

It is unacceptable that the Serious Case Review into this tragic and terrible case has been found inadequate so I am also today directing Haringey Council, under Section 7A of the Local Authority Social Services Act 1970, to appoint a new and independent Chair of its Local Safeguarding Children Board.

Mr Graham Badman, who last week retired as director of children's services in Kent, has agreed to take up this post. He will start work this week. I have asked him immediately to begin a new Serious Case Review into the death of Baby P. He will submit the new Serious Case Review to Ofsted by the end of February for evaluation. And he will publish the executive summary of the new Serious Case Review – which must provide a comprehensive and fair summary of the full Serious Case Review – by the end of March.

This new Serious Case Review will require the commissioning of new management reports from – and the co-operation of – all agencies involved in Child Protection in Haringey. And all agencies must also now implement the wider recommendations made in the Inspectors' report.

The Health Secretary is therefore announcing this afternoon that the Healthcare Commission will undertake an analysis of whether national Child Protection standards are being applied as vigorously as they should be, while the Chief Executive of the NHS will also ask all NHS organisations to review their Child Protection arrangements. And I am pleased that both the Health Secretary and Police Minister Vernon Coaker are also making it clear that the Healthcare Commission and the Metropolitan Police will co-operate fully with the new Serious Case Review.

With these immediate leadership and management changes, with the full implementation of all of the Inspectors' recommendations and with the new Serious Case review, I believe that we can now address the deep-rooted and fundamental failings that have been identified in the tragic case of Baby P and more widely in Haringey.

When I met with the Chief Inspector this morning, she told me that in her judgment the failings in management, oversight and practice identified by the Inspectors' report in Haringey are "exceptional", but this is no reason for complacency. As I told the House of Commons in my statement of 20 November, there is more we must do now and in the coming months to ensure that Child Protection arrangements are effective everywhere.

It is now just over five years since we published Every Child Matters in response to the Victoria Climbié Inquiry, chaired by Lord Laming. And while Lord Laming himself and the Joint Chief Inspectors in their report to me in July have said these reforms have significantly strengthened the framework for safeguarding children, there is still much work to do to ensure these reforms are being implemented robustly in every area.

Ofsted is today publishing its first evaluation of Serious Case Reviews, which highlights that there is variable quality across the country in conducting these Serious Case Reviews. And Lord Laming has today written to me with a progress report and to set out his initial recommendations to strengthen the Serious Case Review process, including that all Serious Case Reviews are independently chaired.

Lord Laming will set out more details in his February report, but I want to take further action today, so I am asking each Local Safeguarding Children Board responsible for a Serious Case Review which has been judged inadequate to convene a panel to be chaired by an independent person to reconsider the review. I will then seek Ofsted's advice on whether that report satisfactorily addresses the issues rated as inadequate. And this same process will be used for any future

Serious Case Reviews that Ofsted assesses to be inadequate.

Ofsted has also decided that each year they will undertake an unannounced inspection visit of safeguarding practice in every area of the country and where areas have had more than one inadequate Serious Case Review, I will consider whether further action is needed.

I have today written to every Director of Children's Services and Lead Member for Children's Services in the country, enclosing a copy of the Haringey Inspectors' report, to ensure that they are examining their own safeguarding arrangements.

I have also today accepted all of the safeguarding recommendations in the Joint Chief Inspectors' report and published the Government's response.

In his letter, Lord Laming also raises the question of a Public Inquiry into Haringey Children's Services. He says that he has been "struck by the robustness of the foundation on which current Children's Services are based." He sets out his view that a Public Inquiry into the services in Haringey would set back the progress that has been made in many places and divert effort from the actions needed now to keep children safe in Haringey.

I agree with this judgment. For now, our priorities must be to:

Put in place the leadership and management team in Haringey Children's Services that can ensure that vulnerable children in the borough are properly protected

Appoint a new independent chair of the Local Safeguarding Children Board to begin a new Serious Case Review into the death of Baby P

And ensure that action has been taken across the country in

response to those Serious Case Reviews that have been judged to be inadequate.

That is what I have done today.

Nothing we do now can take away the terrible suffering that was inflicted on Baby P during his short life. The sad fact is that, as the Inspectors' report makes clear:

Baby P had been subject to a Child Protection Plan from 22 December 2006, following concerns that he had been abused and neglected. He was still subject to this plan when he died. That is the most serious failing of all.

We will not rest until we have the very best Child Protection arrangements in Haringey and across our country.

The day after she was sacked Sharon Shoesmith left her flat in Holborn and went out for lunch at a nearby Italian restaurant. She said nothing – but her response to her axing lay in the not-too distant future.

10

CHANGES

THE DUST had hardly settled on Sharon Shoesmith's sacking when the new broom replacing her was announced: Peter Lewis, the Director of Children's Services at nearby Enfield, was to take over. His appointment by Ed Balls was to start on 1 January and he was reported to be on a salary of £200,000 a year for taking on the job.

He pledged to work to bring 'stability and renewed confidence', adding, 'I do not underestimate the challenges associated with taking on this role but I believe we can build a strong team at Haringey and deliver better lives for local children and young people. I look forward to taking up the new job in January and discussing with the staff and other organisations in Haringey how we can learn from the past and improve services for the future.

'Safeguarding is the responsibility of the whole borough, not any one team or person,' he continued. 'Therefore the role of director of Children's Services requires the ability to bring lots of different people and services together to focus on the needs of children and young people.'

Lewis had been director of children's services in Enfield since February 2004. Ed Balls commented: 'Peter Lewis has great experience and an excellent reputation. I am confident that he will provide the strong leadership which is needed to improve outcomes for children and young people in Haringey.

In fact, Peter Lewis hardly had time to get his feet under the desk before the news broke that Sharon Shoesmith had decided to take legal action over her dismissal. If successful, she stood to win over £100,000 in lieu of a year's notice and up to £63,000 for unfair dismissal.

Lynne Featherstone, the local MP and a leading critic of Haringey's handling of the case, remarked: 'Sharon Shoesmith should not receive a penny. I hope she doesn't succeed with this appeal. This has been a defining moment when serious failure was not rewarded and if that were to be reversed it would be a green light for people to fail with impunity. It is important to remember that when Haringey sacked her, they said there had been "a fundamental loss of trust and confidence in Ms Shoesmith."'

Ed Balls, described the department run by Mrs Shoesmith as 'not fit for purpose.' But one employment lawyer said: 'It is a fundamental principle of justice that both sides in an employment dispute must be allowed to have their say.

'If she was not given that chance then she may have a case that the council did not follow due process. Otherwise she could argue that she was not guilty of the kind of gross misconduct which would justify immediate termination without compensation.'

He added: 'It is a very unfortunate and unusual case. Ed Balls was not her employer, the Government was not her employer, and yet Mr Balls appears to have directed that she should not be given any payment before an investigation was carried out by her employer.'

Michael Gove's reaction was: 'There should be no reward for failure. Rather than compensating the individuals who presided over this tragedy, we should be pursuing those still being paid by the taxpayer who share responsibility for what went wrong.'

One source close to Shoesmith said: 'She is basing her appeal on the grounds that the panel failed to apply the law properly, and failed to check whether the findings of the highly critical report were true.'

The appeal in front of three councillors lasted three days but she was eventually unsuccessful and a council spokesman stated: 'Ms Shoesmith will not be returning to work in Haringey. She will not receive any compensation package. She will not receive any payment in lieu of notice.'

At approximately the same time as Shoesmith was losing her appeal, her replacement Peter Lewis wrote to his counterparts in the London area asking for help. He said that Haringey had a shortage of skilled staff to address a 'pinch point' in assessing suspected child abuse cases: 'If each of the 30 other boroughs could provide one good quality person for a period of four weeks, that would make a difference. Please give this serious and careful consideration.'

A Haringey Council spokesman added: 'We are in contact with a number of organisations, including councils and charities, to take forward our improvement work and have already received support from other local authorities. We want to ensure that sufficient staffing resources are available to deliver Social Care services.'

At some stage Sharon Shoesmith had to answer all the criticism she had received, and that point was reached in early February 2009.

It's hardly surprising that she chose the *Guardian* newspaper as one of her platforms – it is linked so closely with social workers that it is known as their 'bible' – it would have been astonishing if she had done otherwise and given that many other newspapers had turned her into a monster figure, it was a natural choice.

The other outlet for her reaction to the fury unleashed was the weekend edition of *Woman's Hour* on Radio 4 where she was interviewed by Jenni Murray. She didn't pull any punches in her opinion of Mr Balls, she accused him of 'breathtaking recklessness' in his handling of the matter, saying his actions had fuelled a blame culture that had left social workers demoralised and put child safety procedures at risk.

She also pointed a finger at what she felt was political opportunism and press hysteria, which created 'a local tragedy and a national catastrophe.'

Explaining for the first time some of the background to her hearing of the death of Baby P, Shoesmith said that in her old job she would be told about the death of every child in the borough of Haringey: 'But when you get a child who's died, is known to us, is on our at Risk Register, that's the biggest horror that could have been and we knew the size of that.'

It was Friday, 3 August when she first heard and she called the Leader of the Council, George Meehan, who was on holiday and they both realised the seriousness of the situation immediately. She didn't ring Liz Santry as she too was away, something she later regretted as Ms Santry heard of the death on a news bulletin. The social worker involved was informed of what had happened and so too was Ofsted. All the information about Peter was then put in a secure room, she said.

At the time she could have left her post immediately as she was being headhunted for chief executive jobs elsewhere, she told the *Guardian*, but, 'I always, always, always felt that that was the last thing that I was going to do; that that was the weakest thing that I could do. That was betrayal, to walk away from the council and leave them to handle this.

'Other social workers knew the size of this and if you're not careful, you begin to lose your staff and the department could go into meltdown basically, and could go into being a very unsafe place.'

One of the main criticisms of Shoesmith had been that she had 'investigated herself' in the Haringey Inquiry into Baby P's death, an accusation she strongly rejected: 'It is on record that some 70%-plus of directors of children's services chaired their local safeguarding children boards and if you look at London, I'm told at the time of Baby P's death only 7 of the 32 local authorities had an independent chair... So yes, I chaired it and there's absolutely nothing unusual about that anywhere in the country.

'I was in the room when the police came to tell some of those staff that she [Tracey Connelly] had been charged with murder and I'll remember the scene forever because they simply couldn't believe it.

'One of the huge learning issues I think that comes out of this is they were operating this rule of optimism, that this mother was working with them and there was huge – well, I say there was huge deceit. I don't know to this day what the mother knew and understood either.'

She read transcripts of the trial nightly, she didn't go to the Old Bailey, and had requested specialist training for a press briefing at its end. It was that press conference – the infamous one where she 'wouldn't say sorry' – that catapulted her into notoriety.

'I obviously wasn't looking forward to it, but I felt it was my responsibility to step up to that role, and to explain to the public, try to explain to the public what had happened. And it was a complete disaster, which I fully recognise.

'You know, I've thought and thought about that and I thought, well in some ways we were so sorry and distressed about this, we almost did not say that. Nobody, you know nobody, was more sorry and distressed than I was, to be sitting there telling this to the public through the press representatives,' she told the paper.

She also regretted the moment when she was asked two questions at once, and turned to answer one when the other was 'have you apologised to the father?' 'That was interpreted as a "no". I should have gone back and addressed it, and had I done, I would have said that we'd had good contact with the father. He'd been asked to contribute to the Serious Case Review, if he wished. He did decline. And we also clearly wrote to him and gave him our condolences.'

Shoesmith said that in all other interviews that day she had apologised, but the damage was already done. She continued: 'If you are going to sack every director of every children's service where there is a child death, you're going to turn them over at the rate of a third a year.' And she then added: 'You do consider how to stop it all, you know. You can just walk off the end of the tube platform and stop it all, and I certainly did think about that on occasion, and there was certainly another occasion in the middle of the night when I gathered up all the paracetamol that existed in the house and there was nothing like enough.'

She said that on Friday, 28 November she offered the council her resignation; they even agreed a form of wordage that she was leaving by 'mutual consent', but the decision was quickly overtaken. At 6pm on the Sunday the independent report with its total condemnation was delivered to Balls.

'Of course I expected criticism,' said Shoesmith. 'Nothing is perfect, but not that. And I was really very shocked.' She said that the reference to a conflict of interest discredited her, no feedback had been allowed and she thought it strange that there were no positive elements to it despite positive statements being made during its preparation.

Her first realisation that she was being replaced, she said, was when she saw it announced on the news by Ed Balls on 1 December. She also told the *Guardian* that, contrary to reports of £1 million pensions, she now had nothing – no savings, no income, and no pension.

'I just think it's a huge travesty for Haringey and if there's anything I want to say, it's that they deserve much better than this, because I know who the people are and how they've worked and how they've achieved, and it just has been deeply reckless, breathtakingly reckless, and I don't think people really understood quite what the potential impact could be. And now you've got this, a local tragedy and a national catastrophe.'

On *Weekend Woman's Hour* she said: 'Of course I've been distressed about this, of course I have, and had many sleepless nights over it. But if there's a young person killed through knife crime this weekend, and I hope there isn't, do we expect the borough commander of that London borough to resign? We don't, we don't.'

When interviewer Murray queried the validity of her comparison because a child such as Baby P should be constantly monitored, Shoesmith responded: 'A child is not constantly being observed. When there are visits to a child, you get a snapshot of what you see in that home. I have sat in that room while the independent authors went through the detail of what was seen and what was heard.

'There isn't a video running in that home; there was not a way of knowing that there's a man hiding in the wardrobe, that there's a trench dug out the back garden and there's somebody in it. Of course that goes on. These people were a bit cleverer than that – they were much cleverer than that, actually, in the level of deceit.'

And she added: 'The first time I saw that [Ofsted] report was when it was already published on a website accessible to the public. The first time I knew any inkling of the degree of criticism in it was watching the Secretary of State live on television.'

Reflecting on events, she told Murray: 'Maybe one of the things we misjudged was the public opinion in this: interviewers are going to ask me, "Can you guarantee there won't be any more deaths?" and that's a very difficult question. In many ways I had to answer it honestly and the public didn't want to hear that honest answer.'

She also expanded on her newspaper remarks about taking her own life: 'Without being dramatic, I think when people are in the eye of the storm, as I was, you do consider how you might end it all and of course, I did that. I don't think I would have done, I was still rational, but I certainly had those sorts of thoughts.'

The 55-year-old, who said the first time she saw Baby P was when his picture was in a newspaper, again defended her department over his death: 'Across that period what is important to understand is that social workers or indeed health visitors were not going into a home and seeing a badly injured child, of course they weren't. They were seeing a child where there was some concern, but it wasn't enough. It was enough to arouse their suspicions, but it wasn't enough to meet the threshold for care proceedings.'

In the wake of Shoesmith's interviews, Ed Balls hit back: 'I make no apology for the actions I took in Haringey last December, which I judged absolutely necessary to make sure children in that borough are properly protected. Social workers do an incredibly difficult and sometimes dangerous job every day to keep children safe.

'They are unsung heroes of our country. The actions I have taken to set up the Social Work Taskforce, which will look at improving the training and standing of social workers, to ask Lord Laming to review progress in implementing the Every

Child Matters reforms and to ensure all serious case reviews are independently chaired are all essential to support social workers in the job they do to keep children safe from harm. But when things go wrong, it is vital that we act. And that is why I sent in the independent children's services, police and health inspectors to investigate the situation in Haringey. Their report was devastating and revealed serious failures in the management of Haringey Children's Services.

'I believe that every community, every parent and every social worker would expect me to put the safety of children first. That is what I did – and faced with the same situation again I would have no hesitation in taking exactly the same decisions.

'In Haringey, in particular, it was so important things were working properly, and they weren't. I didn't jump in, even though I was pressed to do so. I waited for an independent report. I sent in inspectors – the experts – to do the work. In a devastating report, they said there were real failures in management in Haringey. In the end, the Director of Children's Services has to take responsibility.'

Among many newspapers, the reaction to Shoesmith was not favourable, and many of them took the same theme.

The *Daily Mail* wrote: ' "No Remorse". In two breathtakingly self-pitying interviews, the council chief at the centre of the Baby P scandal says she is the victim of a media witch-hunt, blames everybody but herself for the furore and still can't bring herself to say one crucial word... sorry.'

The *Mail on Sunday* was in a similar vein: 'The disgraced council boss sacked over the Baby P scandal was criticised yesterday for failing to apologise for the toddler's death during her first interview since her sacking. Instead, Sharon Shoesmith, the former £100,000-a-year head of Haringey council children's services, blamed everyone but herself. Among others, she attacked Ministers for their handling of the affair, accused the Press and public of a witch-hunt and claimed she was blatantly discredited by an independent inquiry. And she described in self-pitying detail the tragedy's toll on herself and her family, causing dismay yesterday among those close to the case.'

A *Sunday Mirror* columnist too was unimpressed: 'You'd think Sharon Shoesmith would have learned to say the word "sorry" by now. But no, the former head of child services at Haringey Council is at it again, blaming everyone else but herself for not protecting tragic Baby P.

'The woman damned by an Ofsted report for her failings and removed from her £100,000 job after refusing to properly apologise or resign now has the audacity to accuse Ed Balls of "breathtaking recklessness".

'If you want the true definition of "breathtaking recklessness", try this for size, Sharon – it's when a baby on your child protection register is found killed in his own home despite having 60 contacts with authorities.'

And the *Sun* said: 'Sharon Shoesmith, the Haringey Baby P boss, gives an interview to social workers' bible the *Guardian* (where else?), whining that she contemplated suicide. Not out of shame for her negligence or failures, but over demands for her resignation.

'This is meant to make us feel sorry for her. But why should we? She was in charge of the department that let Baby P die and she STILL hasn't apologised.'

And it wasn't just the popular press who were critical, either. An editorial in *Children and Young People Now* echoed their remarks: 'Haringey's former director of children's services has now told her side of the Baby P story. Strikingly, three months on, the ability to unequivocally say sorry still eludes Sharon Shoesmith in the interviews that surfaced last weekend.

'With the identity of the mother and partner kept anonymous, her defiance in front of the cameras in defending her service gifted the media a visible target on which to vent the public's rage. It whipped up the storm that precipitated the vile, and wholly unfair, personal abuse against her and that led eventually to Children's Secretary Ed Balls' call for her removal.

'Make no mistake, some sections of the press behaved appallingly towards Shoesmith and yet there is no doubt that the shockwaves over Baby P would be much less severe, had Shoesmith demonstrated a little more humility and humanity.

'While she may still quite justifiably feel no personal or professional culpability over what happened to Baby P, in her position she had to take ultimate responsibility – and that required a clear-cut apology. Leaders in other walks of public life have demonstrated the courage and nous to say sorry when a tragedy or mishap has occurred on their watch.

'It is possible that Shoesmith is still too hardened and raw from the vitriol against her to see this. Given she has given four decades of service to working with children and young people, this is a tragedy in itself.

'Her continual inability to apologise for Baby P is a failure of moral leadership that does the reputation and morale of safeguarding professionals no good.'

11

IT MUST NEVER HAPPEN AGAIN

IN MID-MARCH 2009 Lord Laming delivered his National Child Protection Report, announced in November of the previous year when the scandal of Baby P's death first became public.

In a devastating 98-page critique, he called for a far-reaching package of reforms, from the Cabinet to the most junior frontline social workers who came face-to-face with the cases they had to handle. He expressed frustration at the failure of both the Government and Social Services to implement policies designed to keep children safe, telling professionals to 'just do it'. There were criticisms of the management, training and funding of Child Protection Services and he called for an urgent drive by ministers to bring all councils up to the standards of the best.

Ministers must take immediate action to address 'the inadequacy of the training and supply of frontline social workers' and he demanded that council chief executives should take full responsibility for children's services and criticised the 'wariness' of health workers to get involved in Child Protection.

Lord Laming attacked the heavy caseloads and red tape faced by social workers and said that all staff working with children should have specialist training to help them cope with the rigours of the job. He also criticised the inspection of Social Services and revealed that some police forces had cut Child-Protection work.

Lord Laming said, 'It has been put to me that it is inevitable that some adults, for whatever reason, will deliberately harm children. That may well be so. Nevertheless, it cannot be beyond our wit to put in place ways of identifying early those children at risk of deliberate harm, and to put in place the means of securing their safety and proper development.'

He also stated that the reforms he had ordered after Victoria Climbié's terrible death were still not in place, which meant that nearly 250,000 children were at risk of abuse because Child Protection networks were a shambles and that 55 youngsters had died the previous year at the hands of their parents or someone known to them.

In a shocking condemnation, Lord Laming found staff plagued by low morale, poor supervision, under-funding and inadequate training. He warned that social work had become a 'Cinderella' service that was run by highly paid, but clueless executives and staff were obsessed with form-filling, box-ticking and meeting targets at the expense of protecting at-risk children.

He accused bosses of 'buck-passing' and 'back-covering' when anything went wrong, but pointed out that social workers had no excuse if a child suffered once a protection plan was in place. His report highlighted a lack of information sharing and co-operation between police, hospital staff, schools and social workers.

Lord Laming also attacked a lack of training, which had resulted in inexperienced staff being put in charge of vulnerable youngsters: 'It surprises me that students can complete their training without having any experience of social work, but on the first day after being appointed can inherit a full caseload.' In addition, social workers' judgement was often overshadowed by a complex and lengthy records system.

He urged a Cabinet-led task force to oversee the changes, with major input from the Home Secretary and ministers responsible for schools, health and justice and called for social work chiefs, police commanders and other senior managers to meet to discuss cases of concern. And he also wanted urgent action to tackle under-staffing, with 1 in 10 social worker posts being vacant, turnover rates high and those who stuck at the job reporting a worrying increase in caseloads.

In the Commons Ed Balls accepted all the report's recommendations and said that he was establishing a cross-government unit to improve standards. He announced the appointment of Sir Roger Singleton, former chief executive of Barnardo's, the charity for vulnerable children, to the new post of chief adviser on the safety of children.

A full response to the 58 recommendations was to be published shortly: 'None of Lord Laming's proposals alone could have prevented the death of Baby P, but all of them together add up to a step change in frontline Child Protection. No barrier, no bureaucracy, no buck-passing should ever get in the way of keeping children safe.'

Michael Gove said the report was a 'remarkable indictment of the state of Child Protection in this country,' adding, 'It is scathing about the unwieldy, overly bureaucratic nature of the regime currently in place. It reveals the problems we have with the information technology systems.'

Lord Laming's findings came a week after Sharon Shoesmith again found herself in the headlines when she launched a legal challenge against Ed Balls' role in her dismissal. She filed an application for judicial review at the High Court, challenging the reasonableness of the actions taken by Balls, Haringey Council and Ofsted, and in a separate action lodged an employment tribunal claim in Watford against the council, alleging unfair dismissal. Haringey said it would contest the employment tribunal case 'vigorously', but the children's department said that Mr Balls would not comment on the judicial review to avoid prejudicing the case.

It then emerged that she was in fact seeking compensation in a claim for sexual discrimination by Haringey Council. In unfair dismissal, any potential payout would have been capped at £63,000, but no cap applies to sex discrimination. She put no figure on her claim, but experts said her compensation, which would be paid from taxpayers' cash, could hit £1 million, if her case succeeded.

In the legal papers lodged at the Watford Employment Tribunal, Shoesmith pointed out that following her dismissal, she was replaced by two men and says she was, 'unlawfully discriminated against on the grounds of her gender.' Her papers say: 'The claimant will say she was treated less favourably than a man would have been treated in similar circumstances in that she was summarily dismissed from her job without compensation whereas a man would not have been so dismissed.'

She also revealed that she had suffered 'clinically recognised psychiatric illness and had 'had suicidal thoughts' following her sacking.

Of course, Sharon Shoesmith was not the only one to lose her job.

At the end of February 2009 Dr Jerome Ikwueke, the Haringey GP who saw Baby P in the months leading up to his death, was suspended by the General Medical Council. Although he had twice referred the child to specialists after noticing marks on his body, he was suspended for 18 months by the GMC's interim orders panel while it launched an investigation into his behaviour.

Ikwueke was the second doctor to be suspended over the case. In August 2008, Dr Sabah Al-Zayyat, the consultant paediatrician who missed Peter's broken back, was also suspended for 18 months.

A GMC spokesperson said the decision, 'was necessary for the protection of members of the public and in the public interest.' She added: 'An interim order does not amount to a finding of fact against a doctor. It is a temporary measure put in place while the GMC investigates concerns.'

One local Conservative, however, accused the GMC of conducting a 'witch hunt'.

Justin Hinchcliffe, chair of Tottenham Conservatives and a previous patient of Dr Ikwueke, considered the GP had been made a scapegoat for failings in other parts of the system: 'Dr Ikwueke was the first person to notice and report concerns over

Baby P's injuries. He acted properly in alerting those responsible for Child Protection in the Borough of Haringey.'

Four more heads rolled at the end of April – three council managers and one social worker were sacked by Haringey Council for allegedly failing to prevent Baby P's death.

£80,000-a-year deputy director of children and families Cecilia Hitchen, team manager Gillie Christou, head of safeguarding services Clive Preece and social worker Maria Ward were all dismissed by the council.

A Haringey spokesman said Ms Hitchen was sacked for 'loss of trust and confidence' following the Ofsted report in December 2008, which found 'fundamental failings' in the way vulnerable children were dealt with. Mr Preece was dismissed for allegedly rejecting a plea for Baby P to be taken from his home and placed in care after his mother was arrested on suspicion of child cruelty.

Maria Ward, the social worker in charge of Peter's case, who visited his home 10 times but failed to notice bruises caused by physical abuse were being hidden by chocolate and nappy cream, was also axed and former team manager Gillie Christou was fired for approving the decision to return the child home on the mistaken understanding that a friend of his mother's was living there.

The two women were dismissed for alleged gross misconduct, after having both remained at work since the scandal was disclosed in November 2008.

March and April 2009 saw a constant flow of stories and leaks, all critical of the way that Haringey Council was carrying out its work with children.

The *Mail on Sunday* published details of the first Serious Case

Review overseen by Sharon Shoesmith and claimed that it showed how the council played down the scale of the brutality inflicted. Also that there were grounds for an interim care order to remove the child from his home six months before he died, but nothing was done. The review was completed the previous November, but only a short 'executive summary' had been published.

A Haringey Council spokesman said: 'This leaked document is the November 2008 review that was judged inadequate by Ofsted and the Secretary of State for Children, Schools and Families in December, following an intensive inspection of Child Protection services in Haringey.

'The council and other agencies responsible for safeguarding children have accepted that finding and apologised for the failings in this case.

'A new review into the case was ordered by the Secretary of State, under a new independent chair of the Haringey Local Safeguarding Children Board, Graham Badman. A summary of this review will be published in due course.'

Soon afterwards a further leak, widely reported, said police began an investigation into suspicious bruises on Baby P's head and body in December 2006. However, the case 'drifted' after the detective in charge changed jobs in March and did not pass the case to another officer. The investigation then stalled for four months, which meant that the six-month limit for bringing a charge of common assault had passed. The report suggested that Peter might have been saved, had charges been brought. Certainly, this would have certainly increased the chances that he might have been removed from the family home. Scotland Yard declined to comment.

One final report was to be published early that summer – the one presided over by Graham Badman, which was ordered after the initial review supervised by Shoesmith. Not surprisingly, it too was damning in its findings.

It set out what everyone who had read details of the case knew in their hearts: Baby P's death 'could and should have been prevented', but social workers and other agencies were too eager to keep mother and child together. All those concerned could have stopped the cruelty 'in its tracks at the first serious incident' but their outlook was 'completely inadequate' and Baby P should have been placed in care, found the review carried out by Haringey Local Safeguarding Children Board.

Council workers denied any knowledge of Tracey Connelly's boyfriend, even though her former partner, Baby P's father, had warned them that he had seen him at the family home. Although agencies thought it unlikely the mother was injuring the child, no one took the next step and looked into whether anyone else was involved, the executive summary of the review stated.

Even after Baby P was put under a Child Protection plan, his case was regarded as routine, 'with injuries expected as a matter of course'. The professionals tasked with the boy's protection were 'lacking urgency', 'lacking thoroughness' and 'insufficiently challenging to the parent'.

Referring to the decision to remove a child into care, the review said: 'There will be times when [professionals] have to grasp the nettle, using professional judgment, in the knowledge that they may be proved to be mistaken. Better that than the harm that the child will have to experience instead.'

Graham Badman said: 'I believe the most important lesson

arising from this case is that professionals charged with ensuring child safety must be deeply sceptical of any explanations, justifications or excuses they may hear in connection with the apparent maltreatment of children. If they have any doubt about the cause of physical injuries or what appears to be maltreatment, they should act swiftly and decisively. There are a number of points in this story as it unfolds where you could see care proceedings should have been followed – the thresholds were met. Much more attention should have been paid to the role of this man entering this vulnerable family. Baby P's horrifying death could, and should have been prevented.'

The Serious Case Review said that had doctors, lawyers, police officers and social workers adopted a more urgent, thorough and challenging approach, the case would have been stopped in its tracks at the first serious incident: 'Baby Peter deserved better from the services that were supposed to protect him.'

Mr Badman said the manipulative and deceptive behaviour of the mother was 'no mitigation' for social workers and agencies, and it was important for them to use the 'first-hand evidence of their own eyes' when dealing with such cases.

'Should more attention have been applied to the existence of the man? The answer is an unequivocal "yes,"' he remarked, adding that there was 'an enormous willingness' to believe the mother's stories. 'If you know or suspect that there are injuries that are non-accidental and you don't believe the mother is capable of doing it, then there must have been somebody else.'

Every member of staff in the agencies involved with the case was appropriately qualified and did what was expected of them, but they were operating on the assumption that they could help the family by keeping them together, he said. He added that he thought the result of the review would be that agencies were more willing to 'pick up the phone' to raise concerns.

Social workers failed to take Baby Peter into care despite advice from lawyers that the 'threshold for care proceedings had been met' just after Christmas 2006, the review stated, and in late July 2007 – days before the child's death – another chance to take him into care was missed when the decision was made at a legal planning meeting that his case did not meet the threshold for care proceedings.

The review found an 'over-reliance' on medical and criminal evidence and said that just because a decision was made not to prosecute an individual, this did not mean that injuries should be regarded as uncertain or accidental. Finally, 'The panel concludes that nothing less than injuries that were non-accidental beyond all reasonable doubt would have caused him to be moved to a place of safety. When such injuries did come they were catastrophic, and he died of them.'

Haringey Council leader Claire Kober commented: 'This review clearly shows there were failings by all the agencies involved with Baby Peter. There were opportunities to help this family, which should have been taken. I apologise for those failings.'

Lynne Featherstone MP commented: 'The first Serious Case Review either showed clear incompetence or was a cover-up, this one could not be more different from the first. It says exactly what we should have learnt at the start of this awful tragedy – Haringey Council, health professionals and the police all failed to protect Baby Peter from three individuals who set out to harm him.'

While it is not the purpose of this book to simply reproduce official documents, the Badman report is an exception. It gets to the very heart of why Baby P died and what went wrong among those who should have cared for him. Most importantly, it suggests what should be done to prevent a reoccurrence of such a tragedy.

To that purpose, the sections of the report titled 'Lessons to be Learned', 'Conclusions' and 'Recommendations' are reproduced at length. All are presented in clear, easily accessible writing style and every word is important in understanding the tragedy of the case and thereby perhaps preventing any child suffering so again:

LESSONS TO BE LEARNED

This section outlines the main lessons to be learned which when applied, should prevent significant harm occurring to future children in similar circumstances.

THE NEED FOR AUTHORITATIVE CHILD PROTECTION PRACTICE

The only leverage which the inter-agency response has in a situation in which a child is believed to have been harmed by those unknown is the motivation and sense of responsibility which the parents/carers have for the child. The s.47 (Section 47, Children Act 1989, child protection investigation) enquiries by CYPS (Children and Young People's Service), the investigation by the police, and the child protection conference were all opportunities to discover the extent to which the parents/carers loved the children and were able to demonstrate their responsibility to care for and to protect Peter.

Although perhaps not consciously, a parent/carer in Ms A's [Tracey Connelly] situation is testing the resolve of the safeguarding and child protection systems. She had not yet found it necessary to disclose what had happened to Peter, and in particular who had caused the injuries. From the beginning she was given every indication that she may not need to do so.

Agencies were too willing to believe Ms A's accounts of herself, her care of the children, the composition of her household, and the nature of her friendship network. Such an account may well have proved to be accurate when tested over time, but at that stage it should have been assumed that it might be self-serving. The danger is an over-identification with the service user in a wish to support and protect the child's place in the family. There was already reason to believe that she was not being truthful about the injuries to her child.

Peter was the subject of a child protection conference in December 2006, with injuries so serious that they met the threshold for care proceedings. Although it cannot be known for certain how the injuries occurred, the medical view of the causes of the injuries went as far as it could in offering a non-accidental opinion – and it was gradually discounted. The likely explanation is that the injuries were not regarded as sufficiently serious and that there was an over-identification with the parent whose account of possible explanations was perceived to be plausible. Too little significance was given to

Ms A's own childhood experience of serious physical and emotional abuse and the possible impact of it both on her own parenting and her ability to manipulate the system.

Neither the paediatrician nor a representative of the hospital medical team was at the child protection conference to advocate for the reality of the child's injuries. There was the real possibility that force had been used on Peter by an adult, that nobody was accepting responsibility, and that somebody was covering up. That was the reasonable inference and it should have guided the initial inter-agency response. It is difficult to understand how Peter could be returned to the family home after he has been seriously injured, possibly deliberately by an adult, and there is no resolution of who did it. It is reasonable to presume that Ms A was hoping to get away without either admitting to it herself or disclosing the identity of the perpetrator. It is the view of the author that just as the services have been testing her, she is testing the resolve of the services.

It is important to reflect on the process which took place at the conference. The majority of the members of the conference were not specialists in child protection. Their function was to bring safeguarding awareness to their daily work with children (e.g. the school) or to work in promoting the children's welfare (e.g. Family Welfare Association). They do not carry the main responsibility for protecting Peter and it was unwise for the conference Chair to give them the responsibility for deciding the basis of the child protection plan. It is the role of Chairs, with their experience and expertise, to guide the members to a conclusion and note where there are any dissenters.

There may not have been sufficient awareness on the part of the participants, and particularly the Chair, of the dynamics of the relationships between the participants, and the part which procedures could play in minimising any adverse effects. Ms A's presence in the meeting would have an influence on the agency representatives, who may feel that they need to protect their relationship with her as they have to work with her in the future. The impact of her presence would be compounded by the fact that she was accompanied by a solicitor. Ms A was apparently a dominating and forceful personality who may have intimidated people in the meeting and certainly had done so outside of it. Most importantly, there was reason to believe that she had not been frank about the injuries to Peter and who had caused them. There is provision to ask a parent to leave a meeting for part of the time, to check that there are not things being held back because of her presence.

Child protection plans were not required for all the children. It is true that no concerns had been expressed by the agencies about the care of the older children, and there was no indication of neglect or of injury when they were examined shortly after Peter's injuries came to light. However, two children were on child protection plans. Either these children were being selected deliberately for maltreatment or they exhibited the vulnerabilities of generally neglectful parenting because they were younger. As the adults had refused to disclose what had happened to Peter, it was reasonable to conclude that all the children could be at risk of significant harm, and all of them should have received the added security of a child protection plan.

The fact that children are on a child protection plan is an important signal to other agencies that they should carefully monitor their welfare. Discriminating between children in this manner can be a way of agencies trying to be fair or to reward the parent by saying that not all her parenting is poor. Not only were all the children experiencing a degree of neglectful care but it can give the wrong message to parents: that they only need to improve their parenting in respect of some of their children.

The components of the child protection plan were never developed, at least in writing. The plan was wrongly conceived and if it was carried out literally then it would not have the desired impact on Ms A's parenting. It was unlikely to prevent further neglect or injuries to Peter if the element which had caused it in the first place was still present. Instead, Peter was regarded as a routine case, with injuries expected as a matter of course, and the case was given the standard and well-tried approach to a family in need of support. Clearly nobody knew what the psycho-social problems/needs possibly were, reflected in Peter's injuries and the neglect of at least one other child.

Placing Peter with a family friend was a clear indication to Ms A that services wanted, if possible, to keep the child with the family, despite his injuries. The injuries are not being taken too seriously. She can reasonably infer that the services need her to care for Peter more than she needs to be honest with them. The implications of the inter-agency and local authority actions appeared to be that this kind of occurrence was not surprising in a family like this. The level of concern was too low; little significance was given to the possibility that a small baby had been injured deliberately, with no account given of it by the adults involved; the expectations of parental care in the family were low; as were the expectations of the services of their own ability to influence events in the family.

What was required was an authoritative approach to the family, with a very tight grip on the intervention. Ms A needed to be challenged and confronted about her poor parenting and generally neglectful approach to the home. Clear targets should have been set with short timescales, particularly in respect to the way she turned the older children out for school, and the upkeep of the home. What needed to be achieved were not those goals in themselves, as important as they were, but understanding her response to the demands placed on her; to discover her motivation and capacity to be a responsible parent. It is likely that these demands would have proved to be stressful for Ms A to achieve. It would have brought to the surface the emotions deriving from her deprived background and would probably be reflected in anger, evasion, resentment and protest. She was angry with the services even though they made no demands on her apart from her time. The passive acceptance of her continued poor parenting was a fundamental problem in the inter-agency approach.

A significant deficit in the first intervention with the family, which was then perpetuated, was the failure to establish the identity of Mr H [Steven Barker], interview him and conduct checks on his background. He was the friend that Ms A claimed was peripheral to the family and had no involvement with the children. One of the potentially dangerous scenarios in child protection is an unrelated man joining a vulnerable single parent family. Ms A's account of his role was accepted too readily. The SCR (Serious Case Review) Panel has agreed that in future it will be the standard practice in relevant cases for both the police and CYPS to interview and thoroughly establish such a man's identity, his background and his involvement with a family. It will be the responsibility of the wider safeguarding agencies to report the existence of these men when they become aware of them.

The incident in March where Ms A struck one of the children on the face, in public with very little provocation, should have been responded to much more authoritatively. The response gave Ms A the wrong message; that the authorities were not too bothered. This was not smacking or considered parental discipline but a shocking loss of control directed to the most vulnerable part of a child's body. It was an assault, and the police should have been informed and a strategy meeting called. Even if that had been a first incident in another family it would have justified a strategy meeting and possible s.47 enquiries.

The value of an unannounced visit by the social worker was demonstrated in bringing the injuries to Peter to light on 1st June. The worker acted correctly and assertively in not accepting Ms A's explanations at face value, and insisting that Peter's injuries be assessed by a doctor at the hospital. Although the view developed that the injuries were inconclusive in respect of being non-accidental, it was reasonable to infer that they were not the result of an accident. Although Ms A had explanations for all the injuries, she had not been sufficiently concerned about them prior to the visit to seek advice and help.

The challenge of the unannounced visit was not to last. The review child protection conference in June followed closely after the injuries to Peter were seen on 1st June. The attendance at the review conference was very poor under any circumstances but given that there had been two sets of serious injuries to Peter since the previous conference in March it is difficult to believe that child protection was given priority in Haringey's child protection and safeguarding systems. Those assigned tasks in the child protection plan should have been invited and present. The FWA (Family Welfare Association) project worker was not invited, nor was she informed of the dates of this or other professionals meetings after May 2007. Of the four protecting agencies only the social workers were represented, with doctors, lawyers and police officers absent. They did not send substitutes and the administration of the conferencing system was so unclear that it is not certain that all were invited. The police did send a written report.

This meeting was an opportunity to review what had happened between March and June; for the doctors to speak of Peter's injuries directly and to advocate for him if necessary. The police believed that the injuries to Peter were non-accidental and they could have strengthened their case for a legal planning meeting by attending. The lawyer could have heard the evidence and discussion first hand from the people present. It was a critical meeting but there is no sense that it was given due weight either in the way that it was organised or in the way that it was responded to.

Another example of the failure of the child protection system to act authoritatively in respect of Ms A and protecting Peter was the failure to arrange an early legal planning meeting to consider the need for care proceedings in respect of Peter. It took seven weeks to arrange the meeting, due to a combination of administrative failures on the part of legal services and a lack of urgency on their part and on the part of the social work managers. To make a wrong decision is regrettable, but to lack urgency in facing up to making it is unacceptable. Legal services now completely accept that and they have put in place systems and safeguards which should prevent it recurring in the future.

Where there is authoritative practice that makes demands on a parent it is the function of family support services to provide the compassion, empathy and encouragement to enable the parent to persevere in meeting those demands. The FWA assumed a family support role in attempting to safeguard Peter and his siblings. They became involved from the first child protection conference and were part of the core group aimed at safeguarding the children and supporting Ms A's parenting. However, despite being in contact with the family until Peter died, FWA were not invited to, or informed about, any professionals meetings after May 2007.

The panel consider that the FWA staff only had a peripheral impact on the functioning of the family. The main problem was that it was never established that there was a basis to work in a family support mode with Ms A. This mode was assumed to be self evident from the beginning, whereas events demonstrate that Ms A marginalized the worker as she did with every agency who was involved with her, including most importantly, the social workers. The only way in which a family support worker could succeed in this case was if the local authority as the lead agency was authoritative, in charge of the intervention, and if the parent understood that the family support agency was their opportunity to improve their parenting.

Part of the terms of reference for this SCR was to examine whether any models of practice had an influence on the way that the case of Peter was managed. A model of practice being partially used in children's social care was Solution Focussed Brief Therapy (SFBT); a method of intervention which attempts to improve the parents' care of their children by emphasising a focus on their strengths. It has a value base as well as its own methods and skills and adherents go through a period of training and their practice skills are mentored.

The senior management of CYPS introduced SFBT as a pilot project within the Safeguarding Team, on the basis of an offer of training which would equip their staff for family support work and create a common ethos around which social workers in the department could work in supporting families. It was seen by some senior managers as appropriate to child protection and at one point they supported a pilot to develop the approach in S.47 enquiries and child protection conferences. Not all staff adopted it, including SW1 (social worker) and TM1 (team manager) in Peter's case, and the child protection advisor considered it unsuitable for child protection in general and certainly for S.47 enquiries and conferences.

It would be reasonable to infer that this approach may have had some influence as it was being piloted in the social work team that was working with the family from February 2007. Their STM was one of the key drivers for the pilot and conducted an interview with Ms A using the approach in March 2007 as part of her own training to complete a Diploma in the approach.

However, there is no evidence from scrutiny of case records or interviews conducted that it had a direct impact on this case or its outcome. The SFBT approach has a place in family work and emphasising the strengths of parents is important, but it is not compatible with the authoritative approach to parents in the protective phase of enquiries, assessment and the child protection conference if children are to be protected. When the social worker, their manager, the conference chair and the core group are confident that the parents are giving genuine cooperation with the staff, then a family support approach alone like this one is appropriate, as long as there is continued awareness that the assumptions may be mistaken.

IMPROVE INTER-AGENCY COMMUNICATION

Nothing illustrates the agencies' failure to communicate effectively more than Ms A's attendance at the Mellow Parenting programme. This health-led programme offered an intensive day-long experience of social learning and support to parents with relationship difficulties with their children. The social workers who commissioned the programme saw Mellow Parenting as an important current arrangement in protecting Peter and the other child on the register, and also for the longer term in helping Ms A to be a more thoughtful parent. The social workers and the programme providers had different expectations of each because they were not clarified, and Peter was left for long periods on the programme days with somebody unknown. There was no arrangement to inform the social worker if Ms A did not attend, and crucially no alert if, when she did attend, Peter did not accompany her. Ms A attended 9 of the 13 sessions with the other child but Peter only accompanied them on 4 of those sessions. Nobody knew who was looking after him on those days when he did not attend.

The failure to offer Peter an early appointment at the CDC (Child Development Centre) was caused in part by a failure to communicate the true position of his risk of harm by those requesting the appointment. CDC were informed that he was on the child protection register and thus subject to a child protection plan, but in addition they should have been told that he was currently subject to s.47 enquiries into recent injuries. This was his status, but he was not regarded as such. The CDC say that if this had been made clear when the team manager pressed for an early appointment, they would have seen Peter within 48 hours. The basis on which he was being referred to the CDC was to rule out an organic reason for his head-banging and head-butting behaviours.

In the view of the SCR panel, the main reasons for which he should have been referred to the CDC was for an assessment of the seriousness of his neglect, the impact of it on his development, and whether it was likely that there was any other explanation for the head-banging and head-butting than the pain and frustration he was experiencing at the hands of those caring for him. Even the family friend noticed that the head-banging disappeared while he was in her care. Given the seriousness of the injuries which Peter had been experiencing all along, the referral looks like casting around for any kind of explanation for his injuries other than that he was being harmed by someone with access to him.

Peter was unwell and miserable at the assessment and there were even visible bruises. The doctor may have meant well in deferring the examination but even without the bruises there can be only one absolute rule when a child subject to a child protection plan presents in this way to a health professional: he must be examined.

ENSURE SAFEGUARDING AWARENESS
IN UNIVERSAL SERVICES

The Children Act 2004 and related guidance under the Government's Every Child Matters agenda emphasises the need for early intervention in the lives of vulnerable children in order to support parents with social needs, so that those needs are addressed early to prevent them from becoming more serious. Every local authority and its children's Partnership or Trust is required to develop local delivery of services, though increasingly multi-disciplinary teams, using the Common Assessment Framework (CAF) and a lead professional. The CAF is not being used by social care staff in Haringey although it has been adopted by education and health services supporting children in universal settings. It is currently used more as a referral tool than it is for assessments.

By any reasonable measure these children were vulnerable: that is, they were entitled to an offer of an assessment to see if the family were in need of additional services. However, there appeared to be a view in the school that the standard of family care of the school-age children was not any different from that of many other families that they knew. This suggests that professional expectations of parents are too low, and that many children may be experiencing unacceptable levels of neglect and emotional deprivation, without testing whether parents would improve their parenting if offered constructive challenge and support.

In many primary care teams there is much closer liaison between health visitors and GPs. In this practice it was exceptionally distant because the arrangements to ensure good communication and a close working relationship between the two professions were not in place. Even without knowing what was to happen subsequently, Ms A's first presentation to the GP about Peter in September 2006 should have suggested that she had anxieties about the care of her son or even fears that she might harm him. The threshold of concern at this point was the vulnerability of the child, and should have led to consideration of the need for a CAF to be undertaken.

The second incident in October 2006 was even more concerning than the first, because the mother was reporting that her child had actually become injured and she wanted him checked by the doctor, although she did not believe that he had suffered any broken bones. Taken together with the first incident, a more concerned view should have been taken of it by the GP. Instead it was treated as a separate coincidental happening, and the mother's account was accepted at face value. The threshold now should have been safeguarding, and it justified the involvement of a colleague, a health visitor, who could make a visit to the home and assess both the home setting and Ms A's relationship with her child. The panel is of the view that the majority of GPs in Haringey would have taken action but there may still be a training need.

Peter was seen with Ms A by his GP on 26th July 2007. The GP has said subsequently that he had considerable misgivings about Peter's appearance and demeanour at that appointment. He felt Peter was in 'a sorry state'. However, he did not take any action to alert others to his concern. He assumed that others would have similar concerns and would be in a better position to take action. He knew that Peter had an appointment at the CDC in a few days.

It is important for professionals to trust their feelings when they perceive children to be suffering, and not make assumptions that others have also perceived it and are better placed to act. It is simpler to lift the telephone than to live with the regret of not having done so.

OVER-RELIANCE ON MEDICAL
AND CRIMINAL EVIDENCE

Whether the parent is prosecuted or not can become conflated with the degree of risk to the child, and whether care proceedings should be initiated. They are different considerations with different thresholds for action. The police are concerned with evidence and place importance on the indications of injuries and the weight which doctors will give to them. Other services can also place too much importance on the medical opinion on the injuries and too much importance on what the police and CPS make of the medical opinion. If these agencies do not prosecute, the injuries can come to be regarded as uncertain and even accidental.

JOINT POLICE AND SOCIAL WORKER
INVESTIGATIONS

The police were only informed and involved at two stages. At other times matters were assessed by the social worker alone or by a doctor alone, denying the police the opportunity to assess whether a crime had been committed and deciding whether to investigate it. This was a wrong emphasis in the context of this case, where injuries reaching the threshold for care proceedings had previously been identified. In relation to the 1st June visit, the police were informed but asked the social worker to assess the situation and inform them of the outcome, when they would decide whether an investigation was justified. This helps to create an unhelpful culture in which other services use discretion about involving the police.

On 11th December, both a social worker and a police officer assessed the situation and the police officer investigated an alleged crime. Subsequently the police officer and social worker jointly interviewed the older children at the school. They did not do it with a video record because at that point no offence had been alleged in respect of them. In cases of alleged maltreatment of children, guidance requires that police and social workers collaborate in bringing together the complementary aspects of evidence-seeking and risk assessment in the interests of protecting the child.

PLACING CHILDREN WITH
FAMILY AND FRIENDS

In the context of a police investigation and s.47 enquiries by the social worker, to place Peter with the family friend was the wrong judgement and gave Ms A the wrong message: that the authorities were not too concerned about the injuries to Peter. However, the managers were literally following the instructions in their own operational guidance of the time, which directs that before using one of the department's foster placements every effort should be made to place the child with family or friends. It does not qualify the guidance for children who are considered to have been the subject of non accidental injuries. The practice should change for these circumstances, as should the guidance.

The family friend was chosen to provide a temporary home for Peter after considering and rejecting Peter's father because Ms A alleged that he had slapped the children in the past. It is not known whether this was clarified with Mr A, to get his view, or whether his wife's version was accepted. Mr A was prepared to take time off from work and to get a reference from his employer. There had been no concerns about his care of the children in the past and he had parental responsibility and the right to care for his son. There should have been very good reasons before refusing his offer of temporary care and his rights should have been explained to him.

THE ROLE OF CARE PROCEEDINGS IN CHILD PROTECTION

There is a balance to be struck between protecting a child from the risk of further significant harm, and undermining his attachment to his family, in particular his parents, but also his siblings. It needs to take into account his age, the seriousness of his injuries, the quality of his relationship to his parents, and the realistic ability of the child protection system to supervise his welfare sufficiently closely to prevent further harm, as well as to improve the parenting. Where the authorities have reason to believe that the parents are not being frank or are not cooperating they should initiate care proceedings either to remove the child from home or to strengthen their position with the child at home. The process of doing so would signal the seriousness of their concerns to the parents. It would also help in a continuing assessment of the parents' motivation and capacity to care for and protect their children.

LACK OF CHALLENGE WHEN
CONDUCTING BASIC INQUIRIES

At no point did it occur to anyone that the injuries to the children were caused by someone else apart from their mother. On the basis of her observed interactions with her children it seemed to be incongruous and unlikely to be her. Her children did not appear to be afraid of her. However, Ms A was an extraordinarily neglectful parent and antagonistic to authority figures, including at the school. In addition one child was acting out in a very unhappy way at school. Ms A could be compliant particularly in her attendance at Mellow Parenting where she attended most of the sessions. The biggest failure of the intervention with Ms A was not to find out how deeply she loved her children or how far she would go out of her way to care for them properly. Very few demands were made on her, either in her care of the children or her care of the home. She was usually in charge of both the family and of the intervention, which was aimed to protect her children and promote their welfare.

Throughout the period covered by this SCR, observations are made of the children and their interaction with each other and with their mother, which were reassuring to the professionals involved with the family. There can be little doubt that these observations were accurate and believed to be genuine. They helped to reduce the concern created when Peter was injured periodically and they undermined resolve when professionals were prepared to act authoritatively. However there can be little doubt now that all the children were being neglected and some of them were being actively abused.

Professionals need to bear in mind that children of this age are very resilient if the abuse is intermittent. Adults define the world for children in a way which makes it difficult for them to envisage another. Quite apart from the injuries to Peter, there were clear indications that all was not well in the care of the children. It is a big decision to remove a child from the care and ambience of their own family, especially when there is no decisive act which makes the decision for the professionals, and they will have to accept the full responsibility themselves. There will be times when they have to grasp the nettle, using professional judgement, in the knowledge that they may be proved to be mistaken. Better that than the harm that the child will have to experience instead.

The Cricklewood episode is an example of Ms A testing out the child protection system and finding it wanting. A number of her children are under child protection plans, she has recently been arrested for allegedly harming Peter, she is the focus of a police investigation, even the social workers are sceptical of her account, and she decamps with all the children without warning or permission. The police are not informed and it does not appear as if she is asked for the address where she is staying so that the authorities locally can establish that the children are safe and whether the account which she had given is true. She is not tested to see if she is a responsible parent and is not warned of the possible consequences when she returns. She did not want to risk not being given permission or the possibility that checks would be made, and she shrewdly judged correctly that there would be no consequences when she returned.

When she returned, Peter had a sore ear. It was assumed that was due to an infection but this was not checked out with the doctors who examined him. No steps were taken to find out if there may have other explanations for the condition. Ms A could have been questioned about the whole episode and checks could have been done to verify her story that she had been looking after an uncle in Cricklewood (it emerged in the course of the later trial that this story was a complete fabrication). Ms A constantly tested the safeguarding and child protection systems and they were always found wanting.

FIRST LINE MANAGEMENT
AND STAFF SUPERVISION

Conducting S.47 enquiries into possible maltreatment of children is complex and potentially stressful work for the social worker. They are acting on behalf of their agency and require the support and supervision of their immediate manager. The manager needs to be both knowledgeable and experienced, and has the advantage of not being embroiled in the immediate tensions and anxieties of the case management. Case supervision and support should be provided at the time it is needed, but also in predictable and regularly arranged episodes so that progress of cases can be reviewed. The manager should also sample the worker's cases as an element of supervision.

The case supervision, particularly for one of the social workers in Peter's case, was ad hoc, inconsistent, and often cancelled. However, even if the supervision had taken place it is unlikely that it would have illuminated the deficiencies in the practice as in this instance the team managers were familiar with the case and themselves had insufficient concerns despite the frequency of injuries to Peter.

Although consultation and supervision is useful in itself in providing support to the practitioner in their work, it will not improve the quality of the practice unless the manager has competent knowledge and skills which are relevant to the requirements of the case.

CONCLUSION

It is reasonable to conclude that, for a case which reflected the highest level of concern that we have for a child's welfare, the interventions were:

- lacking urgency
- lacking thoroughness
- insufficiently challenging to the parent
- lacking action in response to reasonable inference
- insufficiently focussed on the children's welfare

- based on too high a threshold for intervention
- based on expectations that were too low.

The SCR panel is of the view that all staff in every agency involved with Peter and his family were well motivated and concerned to play their part in safeguarding him and supporting Ms A to improve her parenting. They were deemed to be competent in their safeguarding and child protection roles as they understood them to be, based on their experience and qualifications. They had the appropriate qualifications and experience for their roles and were no less qualified and no less experienced than staff in similar roles in other places. However, in this case they did not exercise a strong enough sense of challenge when dealing with Ms A and their practice, both individually and collectively expressed as the culture of safeguarding and child protection at the time, was completely inadequate to meet the challenges presented by the case of Baby Peter.

The uncooperative, anti-social and even dangerous parent/carer is the most difficult challenge for safeguarding and child protection services. The parents/carers may not immediately present as such, and may be superficially compliant, evasive, deceitful, manipulative and untruthful. Practitioners have the difficult job of identifying them among the majority of parents who they encounter, who are merely dysfunctional, anxious and ambivalent. However, in this case the interventions were not sufficiently authoritative by any agency. The authoritative intervention is urgent, thorough, challenging, with a low threshold of concern, keeping the focus on the child, and with high expectations of parents and of what services should expect of themselves.

Everybody working as 'safeguarders' in the safeguarding system, especially those working in the universal services provided by health, education, early years provision and local police, needs to become more aware of the authority in their role, and to use it to safeguard the children as well as to support parents. The mode of relationship with parents, especially on first meeting them, needs to be observing and assessing as well as helpful. Those agency roles which are the protectors – doctors, lawyers, police officers and social workers – need to become much more authoritative both in the initial management of every case with child protection concerns, and in the subsequent child protection plan. It is crucial to be sceptical of the accounts which are given for any maltreatment of the children, and they should be tested thoroughly against the facts. The reasonable inference must be the basis of any action, rather than awaiting care proceedings or prosecution.

Implicit within this report has been the consideration of the resourcing of children's social care in Haringey. It is clear that there were budgetary movements in the periods 2005/06, 2006/07 and 2007/08, but these did not reduce the overall quantum of resource. Within the scope of this review it is difficult to determine whether or not that quantum of resource should have been deployed differently. However, what is clear from the detailed consideration of workload and deployment of frontline staff is that further resources in themselves would not have impacted on the outcome of this case.

It is important to remember that every year many children

die non-accidentally in our country, some of them in similar circumstances to those of Baby Peter. This is not a problem restricted to Haringey and we must learn the lessons. The tragedy is not just that of an individual child's death but the fact that many more children may at this moment be suffering hardship because services do not effect sufficient improvement in their parents. Only a small minority of these children will come forcibly to our notice through their deaths or after serious injury.

Baby Peter's horrifying death could and should have been prevented. If the principles and approaches described in this report had been applied by the four protecting professions, the situation would have been stopped in its tracks at the first serious incident. Peter deserved better from the services which were there to protect him, and they in turn deserved better than the ethos which influenced their work at the time.

In reviewing the services' responses to Baby Peter and his family, the Panel concludes that nothing less than injuries that were non-accidental beyond all reasonable doubt would have caused him to be moved to a place of safety. When such injuries did come they were catastrophic, and he died of them. The Panel deeply regrets that the responses of the services were not sufficiently effective in protecting him and his siblings. The Panel and those independent consultants who contributed to the review have done everything they can to identify the lessons which they believe will significantly reduce the possibility of a similar case happening again. The managers and staff of the agencies involved are fully committed to implementing those lessons.

RECOMMENDATIONS

The LSCB (Local Safeguarding Children Board) and the Partnership must ensure that staff in the four protecting professions – doctors, lawyers, police and social workers – are appropriately trained, individually and together, in the principles and values of the authoritative practice described in this Serious Case Review.

The LSCB and the Partnership must ensure that staff working as 'safeguarders' – the universal services provided by health, education, early years provision and the police – are appropriately trained, individually and together, to recognise the authority in their role and to use it to safeguard children.

The Partnership should give active consideration to the creation of an 'expert pool' from the four protecting agencies. This pool, both virtual and real, will be trained to ensure authoritative knowledge of assessment and intervention. It will be a source of learning, advice and support to ensure effective multi-agency working.

The LSCB will ensure that all agencies fulfil their legal or moral duty to safeguard and promote the welfare of children under s.11 Children Act 2004, and train all staff who have contact with children in safeguarding awareness. The board must seek reports on progress and publish them in their Annual Report.

The LSCB will ensure that the system by which child protection conferences are conducted is changed in order to address the concerns which have emerged from this Serious Case Review. The LSCB will assure itself that conferences are administered efficiently, attended assiduously, managed authoritatively and produce decisions which are child-focussed, with child protection plans that are purposeful and authoritative. The findings should be reported in the LSCB Annual Report.

The LSCB must ensure that children and young people are effectively protected and safeguarded through the regular multi-agency audit of all child protection and safeguarding interventions. It should make report to the Partnership on the quality of their safeguarding and child protection work, and publish the results in its Annual Report.

The Partnership must communicate its passion for an excellent safeguarding service and provide the means for its staff to deliver it. An agency's vision of itself and its sense of drive and purpose is created by its leadership at every level, from the Leader and elected Members down.

The Partnership must fulfil its duty to ensure early intervention in the lives of vulnerable children by addressing with urgency the development of local delivery teams, the widespread use of the Common Assessment Framework (CAF), and the role of the lead professional. It should report on progress to LSCB and invite the Board to audit the safeguarding dimension of the delivery of the services.

The Partnership must challenge the low expectations of parental care widely held by services and assure itself immediately, through audit, that all children subject to child protection investigation and planning are properly protected.

The Local Authority should assure itself that all schools are well trained in the practices associated with welfare and child protection and are clear about their responsibilities in relation to

Every Child Matters. This recommendation equally applies to early years and other educational providers.

The Local Authority should secure an external audit of resources made available to children's services between 2005 and 2008, to satisfy themselves that their expenditure was sufficient to meet the needs of those services and with a view to establishing the appropriate level of resource to meet the requirements of the JAR Action Plan.

Haringey CYPS will ensure that social workers and their managers are trained, supervised and supported to fulfil their statutory role, with the skills to purposefully and authoritatively drive forward child protection plans with the support of other members of the core group.

Haringey CYPS should immediately review the use of Solution Focussed Brief Therapy in their work with families. Its impact on the present ethos in the department should be checked as a part of the review. The department should ensure proper processes are in place for the initiation and evaluation of any change in approach to social work practice.

All agencies offering a family support service to children who are the subject of a child protection plan or to parents of such children, should train their staff in how to work in a complementary role to the social worker who leads and coordinates the child protection plan. The recommendation applies equally to agencies offering parenting programmes and to adult-focussed services.

Haringey LSCB is required to ensure that any outstanding recommendations arising from the previous Serious Case Review (SCR) are fully implemented in accordance with the

Joint Area Review (JAR) Action Plan. The JAR Action Plan will sit alongside and take forward the learning from this Review and the LSCB should scrutinise each development to be assured of its co-ordination, implementation and effectiveness.

Badman Report © Crown Copyright

12

FURTHER ABUSE

I F THE MILLIONS who had been horrified by the death of Baby P thought this gothic tale of menace and brutality could not become worse, they were to be proved wrong on 1 May 2009.

While various reports had been released, enquiries conducted, statements made, pledges pledged and the Great and Good all voiced their views, the reality of the sordid world they were examining and passing judgement on was being described to a jury of eight men and four women at the Old Bailey.

What the jury did not know was that the man and woman whose case they were considering were Baby P's mother and his stepfather. Barker was charged with raping a child and Connelly with child cruelty, a charge she was to be acquitted of.

Tracey Connelly and Steven Barker were tried under false names, Young and Wilson, the first time this had ever happened as pseudonyms were normally reserved for 'supergrasses', in order that their trial would not be prejudiced – although their names had already been published on Internet sites. A reporting ban was also imposed.

There was another 'first' connected with their trial too, a far more disturbing one: the key witness in their trial was the youngest-ever rape victim to give evidence. She was just 4 years old.

The girl, who cannot be named or identified in any way, was just two when Barker raped her, and the fact that a child so young gave evidence was to provoke fierce debate. After a two-week trial, Barker was convicted of her rape and Connelly was acquitted of a child cruelty charge. The reporting ban on the case could therefore be lifted, although the evil duo who stood in the dock were still not named in newspapers or on television.

The girl's filmed police statement was shown to the court and she then faced cross-examination by the defence counsel. The girl was attacked by Barker and her interrogation in court provoked anger afterwards.

Indeed, the tiny tot's method of describing her ordeal seem to emphasise the enormity of the offence committed against her. After initially telling her foster carer about Barker, the girl was still only 3 when she described what happened to a child psychiatrist. She had to use a doll and a teddy bear to help her explain, placing the doll on its stomach on a dolls'-house bed, and then placing the teddy bear face down on top of it.

'It was not nice what he did,' she said. 'He hurt me. It hurt all day.'

It was November 2007 when the girl first told her foster carer Joan Evans that Barker had touched her. One morning, she pointed to her genitals and said Barker, 'does that to me.' Two months later, during a meeting with child psychiatrist Dr Margaret DeJong, she gave a full account. During that meeting in January 2008, she made a series of startling revelations, saying she 'hated' Barker and that he had hurt her. Asked how often it happened, she said, 'lots of times.'

Dr DeJong told the court: 'She said, "He hurt me with his willy." She said it happened lots of times. She said she had told him to stop, but that he never did.'

Police gave her a full medical examination and a 27-minute video of the subsequent interview with family liaison officer Kate Bridget was played to the courtroom, in which the giggling 3-year-old played 'shops' and even hide-and-seek with police. She told police: 'He got hurt me. I was sleeping, he woke me up. He was being naughty again. I was in my 'jamas. He was lying down, like penguins do.'

Asked if she had said anything to Barker, she replied that she had said: 'Don't do it.'

There was no solid forensic evidence so her recollection of the assault was central to the prosecution's case. Although there had been other alleged instances, the prosecution focussed on one in order not to confuse the girl.

She went to the court and was placed in a side room with a court usher for a live cross-examination by video-link. Barristers removed their wigs and introduced themselves by their first names only. The girl met the barristers briefly in the room before they questioned her, but she failed to recognise them when they addressed her from court.

Bernard Richmond QC, defending Barker, asked her if she understood 'fibs'.

Mr Richmond then asked her to remember her November 2007 police meeting during which she shook her head when questioned about abuse. The girl fell silent when the defence lawyer asked her why this was so. Mr Richmond asked her further questions and then said: 'He never touched you, did he? Did he?'

The girl gave a tiny shake of her head. And Mr Richmond asked: 'Was it something someone told you to say? Was it something you made up?'

Eventually she replied: 'I just…' and then went silent again.

Mr Richmond continued: 'I have to ask you one more time: he didn't touch you, did he? We have to have an answer. He didn't touch you, did he? I have to wait until I get your answer, so I can't ask any more questions. He didn't touch you, did he?'

After a five-minute break, Mr Richmond then asked the child: 'What is truth?' At this, the little girl became upset and wiped her face with her hands. He was unable to get any further answers.

At a later hearing which was part of mitigation on behalf of his client, Mr Richmond was to say: 'The cross-examination of a 4-year-old victim of a sexual allegation is one of the most intense and difficult tasks to ever fall to an advocate. We do not pick and choose our cases. We are instructed and it is our duty and privilege to be available to everyone in need of us. Once we are engaged, our duties are clear and established by rules. We must test the evidence against our client and must put inconsistencies to the witness, however young. This case involved putting to her that she was not telling the truth and that these events never happened. Currently in law there is no other method available to us other than cross-examination by video-link following the briefest of introductions. Had there been a more relaxed method, we would have encouraged it and I am sure your lordship would have granted it. There has been some comment that the examination was not appropriate. It is not for me to determine what system can be used in cross-examining children. One can only hope that a more appropriate system will come into play.'

Paul Mendelle, QC, defending Connelly – who was found not guilty on a cruelty charge – had his questions met by nods, shrugs and silences from the little girl.

Prosecutor Sally O'Neill QC said the girl had been confused by their complex questions and was too upset to describe her ordeal. The QC also told the jury: 'Young she may be, indistinct at times certainly, but she was quite clear in what she was saying to the police.'

Although there was fury over her ordeal in court, it was essential that the girl gave evidence as the prosecution case depended on what she had to say, even though she was so young.

After the case, Detective Chief Inspector Graham Grant of Scotland Yard's Child Abuse Investigation Command said: 'It is telling that this man denied rape and in doing so forced a very young and vulnerable child to endure a daunting criminal trial at the Old Bailey. It is also humbling to be involved in a case which relied on the testimony of such a young and violated child.

'Her resilience is extraordinary and I sincerely hope that she will be able to lead a happy and fulfilled life. This case has shocked everyone to the core.'

Andrew Flanagan, chief executive of the children's charity NSPCC, remarked: 'The brutal death of Baby Peter and the rape of a 2-year-old girl are among the most heinous crimes against small children we have ever seen. They leave all decent people bewildered and revolted.'

But there was concern about a child so young being cross-examined.

Carolyn Hamilton, director of the Children's Legal Centre, said that she would be contacting the Ministry for Justice to seek a change to the guidelines: 'A court building, a side room with a live link, is just not suitable for young children to be questioned in by a strange person, even if they take their wig off,' she commented. 'The questions only seemed to succeed in tying the child up in knots. Of course defence counsel have to do their job, but this is not a way to elicit the truth.'

Meanwhile, Barbara Esam, a lawyer at the NSPCC charity, urged courts to consider the use of intermediaries to put questions to children in terms they understood.

Police and prosecution sources also admitted that they were 'shocked' at the way that the girl was dealt with during her court ordeal.

Detective Superintendent Caroline Bates, from the Child Abuse Investigation Unit, said: 'I do not think some styles of cross-examination are appropriate for a child that is this young, but I accept there is no guidance because this is new territory.'

Soon afterwards it was revealed that Barker might appeal against his conviction, with legal sources quoted as saying any possible appeal could focus on the age of his victim, the key witness, in that she was too young to give evidence.

A spokesman for his lawyers said: 'We will go through the process with this client as we do with every client. We presented his defence fearlessly as we are required to do so by the rules and now we will consider the possibilities with him as to any appeal as we do with all defendants.'

But it was to be another three weeks before the sentencing of the trio who had caused Peter so much agony. In that time, further measures were announced to prevent the tragedy ever happening again.

The government announced a £58 million series of steps that they hoped would 'transform' Social Services in the wake of the Baby P scandal. Ed Balls outlined a six-point plan to improve services in response to Lord Laming's independent report.

Mr Balls said he was committed to ensuring 'greater openness', enabling the public to scrutinise Child Protection agencies better and the government would also invest more in training and support for frontline services. He said that the reforms were particularly aimed at 'backing' the good work that is done in social work and attracting good candidates to the profession.

Announcing the plan, he said: 'Our ambition is for social work to be a high-quality profession, with the confidence and support of the public, but to do this we must give social workers the training and support they need to develop,' adding that he had been advised to make the system less 'clunky'.

Days after Barker's conviction, the action plan changes to the Apprenticeships, Skills, Children and Learning Bill were presented. Ed Balls added: 'No single measure can take away the suffering of children which we have seen very graphically in recent days, but we believe what Lord Laming is proposing can help improve child safety.'

The minister did not say whether the reforms could prevent a repeat of the Baby P incident, but: 'When things do go wrong, it is important we act in a tough and robust way, but also that we recognise the job done every day by social workers around the country.'

The £58 million funding was to be distributed as follows:

- Sponsoring 200 university places so high-achieving graduates could convert to social work;
- Funding recruitment campaigns to tempt back social workers who had left the profession;
- Launching a newly qualified social worker support programme for all new practitioners joining statutory and voluntary services that September;
- Funding a new practice-based Masters degree in social work to start in early 2011, so that practitioners could continue to develop;
- Establishing a new advanced social work professional status programme to help experienced social workers stay on the front line.

Under the reforms, the government also promised to overhaul the Integrated Children's System (ICS), the electronic case management system for children's social work. Mr Balls said his department was responding to calls for the ICS to be made 'less clunky and bureaucratic'.

There was one more report to be made public in the wake of

Baby P's death. Although the list seems of such enquiries is seemingly never-ending, they are essential reading if tragedies such as Penshurt Road are to be avoided, or at the very least, reduced in number in the future. This time it was to be the turn of the Care Quality Commission, the independent regulator of health and social care in England. Their findings had not been made public because of the ongoing legal proceedings, but by mid-May this was no longer the case.

Although we have already touched on many of the matters they raise, it was the medical treatment Peter did, or did not, receive that was put under the microscope and their report listed the 30-plus occasions in his short life in which he encountered medical staff.

Like the Ofsted, Badman and Laming verdicts, it deserves to be examined in detail for the improvements that it can bring to the welfare of the nation's at-risk children. Again, it makes chilling reading as it discloses that health workers missed dozens of opportunities to identify abuse being suffered by Baby P before his death because of 'systemic failings' in his care.

The inquiry into NHS failings concluded doctors and other health professionals had numerous contact with the boy but missed every chance to raise the alarm.

Any one of these professionals could have picked up that he was being abused, had they had been 'particularly vigilant' and had they gone 'beyond what was required' by the system, the health regulator said.

The Commission examined the actions of the four NHS trusts in London involved and found a 'catalogue of errors' including chronic staff shortages, inadequate training, long delays in seeing the child and poor communication between health workers, police and Social Services.

Concerns were also raised about the performance of the four trusts: North Middlesex University Hospital NHS Trust, Haringey Teaching Primary Care Trust, Great Ormond Street Hospital for Children NHS Trust and Whittington Hospital NHS Trust.

In the public release about its investigation, the Commission stated:

> It [the report] highlights improvements including measures to ensure that medical staff have a child's background medical notes when treating or assessing them. Steps have also been taken to ensure that a social worker is present at child protection assessments.

But the report also stated that more work needed to be done in areas such as ensuring sufficient staffing levels, improving attendance of healthcare staff at Child Protection case conferences and addressing communication problems, particularly when making referrals.

Speaking about the NHS trusts involved in the Baby Peter case, CQC Chief Executive Cynthia Bower commented: 'This is a story about the failure of basic systems. There were clear reasons to have concern for this child, but the response was simply not fast enough or smart enough. The NHS must accept its share of the responsibility.

'The process was too slow. Professionals were not armed with information that might have set alarm bells ringing. Staffing levels were not adequate and the right training was not universally in place. Social care and healthcare were not working together as they should. Concerns were not properly identified, heard or acted upon.

'The NHS trusts involved have already responded robustly and made clear improvements but there remain significant further steps that must be taken. We must get to a position where we can say everything possible is being done to prevent a recurrence.'

She added: 'It is imperative to ensure lessons are learnt across the country, as well as in north London. We are concerned that NHS trusts don't always know whether they are doing the right things to safeguard children. Our national review will check what information trust boards use to assure themselves they are getting it right. We will not hesitate to use our powers if we find trusts are not doing enough to ensure appropriate safeguarding procedures are in place.'

The report continued:

The Commission's report identifies the following systemic failings:

- Poor communication between health professionals and across agencies, such as social services and the police, meant that urgent action to protect Peter was not taken. For example: the consultant who saw Peter two days before his death did not have any contact with his social worker; health professionals did not always attend child protection conferences to discuss Peter's case; poor completion of child protection forms by some health professionals meant that social care staff were not always aware of their concerns.

- Staff caring for Peter did not always follow child protection procedures. For example: when he was discharged from North Middlesex Hospital in April 2007, no formal discussion was held to escalate concerns, despite him being on the child protection register; there was an absence of bone and skeletal surveys which could have provided a clearer picture of the nature of injuries; staff use of parallel growth charts in the monitoring of Peter's development was not routinely documented, despite ongoing developmental concerns.

- Poor recruitment practices and lack of specific training meant that some staff were inexperienced in child protection. Some staff appointed by GOSH to posts at Haringey PCT were appointed despite not having the required experience in child protection that would be expected for certain posts. They also did not receive appropriate training to develop this knowledge following their appointment.

- Shortages in staffing at St Ann's Hospital, where Peter had his paediatric assessment, led to delays in seeing children. This included shortages in consultants, nurses and administrative staff. At the time of Peter's assessment at St Ann's Hospital on 1 August 2007, there should have been four consultants in post, but there were only two.

- There were failings in governance systems in three of the trusts concerned. Healthcare professionals at North Middlesex Hospital were not always clear on who was responsible for following up child protection referrals, for example, they sometimes relied on social services staff to initiate communication after faxing a referral through. Staff also reported a lack of safeguarding supervision which would have helped ensure that they were clear about their roles and responsibilities in relation to safeguarding children.'

The report continued:

Action Taken By Trusts After Baby Peter's Death...

Staff from the Care Quality Commission's predecessor, the Healthcare Commission, visited the trusts to check what actions had been taken since the failings were identified. They also met with key staff to assess how effective the safeguarding processes are at each trust.

They found that since the death of Peter the trusts had:

- Increased the number of consultants at St Ann's Hospital from two to four, including a named doctor in child protection.
- Made sure background notes are always available prior to an assessment at St Ann's Hospital (commissioned by Haringey PCT).
- Ensured that when a child is referred for a child protection assessment a social worker is present. Although the Commission noted that it was frequently not the child's allocated social worker and therefore often has limited knowledge of the child.
- Updated the shared policy for prioritising and progressing referrals quickly to avoid delays.
- Updated staff training to make sure it complies with safeguarding guidance.

- Established a jointly managed paediatric service at North Middlesex Hospital NHS Trust and Haringey Child Health Services to encourage joint working and sharing of information.

Remaining Shortfalls And Action Being Taken...

The report also makes recommendations to address remaining shortfalls. Although the publication of the report was delayed to prevent any prejudicial effect it may have had on a related court case, the report findings and recommendations were shared with the four trusts in March so they could begin to take action in the following areas:

Some staff at North Middlesex Hospital NHS Trust were still not clear about who is responsible for following up child protection referrals to social services. The report recommended all four trusts should establish clear communication and working arrangements with social services departments. In particular they should ensure contact between agencies is established immediately once a referral is made. GOSH and North Middlesex University Hospital have since developed a cross-agency pilot scheme for new referral systems, but more work is needed to develop and roll out an effective permanent system.

The attendance of healthcare professionals from North Middlesex University Hospital and Haringey PCT at child protection case conferences was not good enough. Some staff at Haringey PCT also said they were not currently receiving any form of safeguarding supervision from a designated or named doctor for safeguarding. The report recommended that boards of all four trusts must assure themselves that these issues are addressed. The trusts have started to address these areas, with many staff now receiving supervision by a designated doctor or nurse at North Middlesex University Hospital, and provision is in place at Whittington Hospital to ensure there is always a member of staff present at a case conference. Trusts need to maintain their focus on these areas as there is still work to do.

The A&E service for children at North Middlesex Hospital NHS Trust was perceived by some staff to be potentially vulnerable as there was no paediatric department after 7pm. North Middlesex University Hospital paediatric A&E is now open 24 hours a day, seven days a week. There remains only one consultant on call for the whole paediatric service after 5pm and at weekends, but there is an adequate complement of other appropriate staff, such as children's nurses and registrars to run the service.

The report recommended Haringey PCT and North Middlesex Hospital must work with GOSH to ensure they have a sufficient number of appropriately qualified paediatric staff. All four trusts should also ensure their staff are clear about child protection procedures and receive safeguarding training to an appropriate level. The trusts have since begun to address shortfalls in staff training where necessary, but more can be done to ensure more people are trained to an appropriate standard.

Haringey PCT is still under-staffed in terms of health visitors, school nurses and support staff. In addition, the report recommended that GOSH must review the consultant cover at St Ann's Hospital to make sure it is adequate. GOSH has made efforts to address this and recognises the need to recruit an academic paediatric consultant. However, the service remains understaffed. GOSH has moved child protection assessments from St Ann's to North Middlesex, where there is better provision of paediatric services.

The trusts involved in the review were required to produce action plans to address the remaining shortfalls. The CQC says although the trusts have already made progress against the report's recommendations, there is still some way to go. It will work with NHS London, the strategic health authority, to monitor trusts' progress.

In order to ensure progress continues, the CQC will be requesting the trusts to provide evidence of implementing the relevant recommendations in six months time. The follow-up may also involve revisiting the four trusts in order to observe how new procedures and policies are working in practice.'

In conclusion, the report added:

CQC's National Review of Safeguarding

As part of its national review of NHS safeguarding arrangements, the CQC has asked all trusts in England to describe what arrangements they have in place to ensure they have effective child protection systems, in line with government core standards and national statutory guidance.

The CQC is concerned that three of the NHS organisations involved in the care of Baby Peter stated that they fully complied with standards for protecting children when this was clearly not the case. It may be that trusts are insufficiently rigorous about ensuring their safeguarding practices are robust and may not be collecting sufficient information to support their declarations.

The CQC's review will look at governance, training and staffing, as well as how individual cases are handled. It will also look at how healthcare organisations work in partnership with others.'

Yet again, this was a chilling indictment of what had gone wrong. A cynic might say in this report, as in so many others, it was perhaps easier to list what had gone right.

The report also recorded all the encounters that Baby P had with doctors, nurses and health visitors before his death. As happens so often throughout the course of this distressing story, it makes one shake one's head in disbelief:

- Six visits to an acute hospital (excluding his birth and death), two to the North Middlesex University Hospital in Edmonton, north London, one to the Whittington Hospital in Archway, north London, and three out-patient appointments.
- Fourteen visits to his family's GP practice.
- One visit to the specialist child health clinic at St Ann's Hospital in Tottenham, north London, two days before he died.
- Five visits by a health visitor to Baby P's home.
- Six visits to the child health visit.
- Two visits to walk-in centres.
- One contact with a midwife.

In addition, his mother saw a mental health worker 16 times and attended parenting advice sessions a total of 9 times, 5 of them with Baby P.

And so another report, yet more condemnation – this time for, among others, Great Ormond Street, a name synonymous with caring for children since Victorian times. The recriminations seemed endless.

Yet more recriminations were in store when Connelly and the Barker brothers were finally told their sentences at the end of May 2009.

13

THE TRIAL

THERE IS ONE central figure so far in the story of Peter Connelly's life that we have not dealt with in any detail – his father. Not the gigantic, illiterate monster of a 'step-father', who came to live in that anonymous street in Tottenham and subsequently wreaked havoc, but Peter's natural father.

There is so much that one might say about him, but for legal reasons it must at this moment remain unsaid for he can neither be named nor identified. However, through statements made in public and on occasions, through the observations of friends that have been openly recorded, he has made clear the anguish that he went through.

His first heartbreaking cry was in November 2008 when the case (known then as 'Baby P') first entered the public conscience and the frightening description of his son's life and death became known. He made the world aware of his torment when he said, after the verdicts on Connelly and the brothers were reached:

I wish to make a short statement to give my reaction to the verdicts following the death of my son, P. The verdicts will help to bring closure for what has been a very traumatic time for me, P's family and indeed all those who knew and were close to him. P was a bouncing 17-month-old boy. I loved him deeply. I remember how he used to run up to me... or when he was in his pram he would bounce up and down until I took him out, giving me hugs and kisses. Those who systematically tortured P and killed him kept it a secret. Not just from me but from all the people who visited the house up until P's death. Even after he died, they lied to cover up their abuse. I would like to thank the police for their efforts in obtaining the evidence to bring a conclusion to this case. I would also like to thank the social workers who have been involved since P's death. They have acted with professionalism and courtesy.

Finally, I wish to thank my family and friends, who have given me comfort and support during this traumatic time. At this stage, I intend to make no further comment. I would ask you to respect my privacy and that of my family. Please allow us to get on with our lives and rebuild our futures.

And then there was an understandable public silence in his part, officially at least, for six months until 21 May when sentence was about to be passed on his former wife and Peter's two other tormentors.

Peter's father's earlier remarks were heartbreaking, yet they seemed as nothing compared with the torment he laid bare that day in May. Many in the Old Bailey, including jurors from the original November hearing who had been invited back, wept as the middle-aged man told his story, read by prosecuting QC, Sally O'Neill. (It is important to remember that in May, it was still not permitted to name Tracey Connelly and Steven Barker.)

The tortured father admitted that since his son's death he felt that he had been living a nightmare. 'My only son must have suffered weeks, if not months of pain, fear and loneliness, with nobody to help or comfort him,' he said. 'No human being, and especially a child, deserves to suffer like Peter suffered.'

He described the day he heard of his child's death: 'I received a telephone call from [Connelly]… she told me he was on his way to hospital and was experiencing breathing difficulties.'

The father ran to his nearest taxi office, but they had no drivers free and so he jumped onto a bus to the next nearest taxi rank to find a driver to take him to the hospital.

'I received a second call from [Connelly], who told me Peter was not breathing. I was frantic with worry and felt an overwhelming need to be with Peter.'

Arriving at the hospital, he pushed his way past the queue at the entrance to Casualty and was then taken the to the resuscitation area.

'I saw his little limp body just laying there, naked except for a nappy. I could not believe what was happening, I could not believe that was my son.

'He appeared to be asleep and I just wanted to pick him up and take him home. There was nothing I could do for him… all I could do was kiss his forehead and say goodbye. My son was gone forever.'

He told the court that he had been delighted to learn that he was having a son and was present at the boy's birth: 'Having a boy meant the world to me, the thought of having a son to continue the family name was a source of great pleasure... Peter was a bright and bubbly child, who was always smiling. He was such an adorable, lovely little boy; he loved to be cuddled and tickled, his laughter and smile could not help but make anyone in his presence feel happy.'

The father then described how his marriage broke up and he was forced to leave the family home when Peter was just five months old. He continued to see his son and described the last time he looked after him, which was on the weekend before his death. By then Peter had been subjected to more than eight months of violent abuse at the hands of his stepfather.

'Peter had come to stay with me over the weekend,' he recalled. 'When I returned Peter to [Connelly], I remember him screaming and shouting, "Daddy, Daddy!" so much that [Connelly] actually brought him back to me to say goodbye again and give him a cuddle.

'I have to live now with the knowledge that Peter was actually screaming for me to help him; he did not want to go home because this was a place that he associated with pain and suffering.'

In his full statement, the father said that initially he assumed his little boy had been a victim of cot death: 'I recall [Connelly] saying, "I'm sorry, I'm sorry" and "They'll blame me for all this," and I instinctively tried to reassure her.

'Even when she was arrested the true nature of what had happened did not occur to me. Not until a week later did I learn of the horrific injuries, which had been inflicted on my little Peter.

'It is one thing to lose a child but to learn your child has been the victim of such appalling cruelty is something I shall never come to terms with. I can only describe it as total devastation, an all-consuming pain, which is both mental and physical.'

He ended his statement by reflecting on his great loss: 'Like all fathers I had imagined watching my son grow up, playing football with him, taking him to see Arsenal play, watching him open his Christmas and birthday presents and just develop as a person. All that has been taken from me.'

The father, who also attacked the lack of remorse shown by Connelly and the Barker brothers, added, 'How do you begin to describe the day your son dies and your entire life is changed beyond all recognition? In the days after Peter's death, my life became a living nightmare. When I then discovered the catalogue of injuries inflicted on Peter, I felt overwhelmed. I just could not comprehend that my son's ribs had been fractured, his ear pulled off, his nails pulled out, his tooth knocked into his stomach and his back broken.

'My only son must have suffered weeks, if not months of pain, fear and loneliness. No human being, especially a child, deserves to suffer like that. It is one thing to lose a child, but to learn your child has been the victim of such appalling cruelty is something I shall never come to terms with. I can only describe it as total devastation and all-consuming pain.'

After first assuming Peter's death was a cot death case and reassuring his wife that her arrest was normal procedure, a week later after he was told of the catalogue of injuries that his son had suffered: 'I felt overwhelmed with a mixture of intense anger, sadness and total depression.'

As well as hearing that traumatic statement from the father, Judge Stephen Kramer also heard mitigation from the trio's barristers, whose duty it was to speak on their client's behalf prior to sentencing.

Paul Mendelle QC, for Connelly, said that his client was an 'immature and uneducated woman' but not 'a cruel mother', that she was not the main abuser and he blamed Steven Barker. However, he added that she had already suffered at the hands of her fellow prisoners. In prison she had been moved to solitary confinement for her own safety because of 'the sanctimonious attitude of those who rob, steal, rape and kill, yet somehow regard themselves as morally superior to an inadequate mother who allowed herself to fall in love with the wrong man.'

Bernard Richmond QC, for Steven Barker, said his client had the lowest IQ of all the defendants and that, in taking on the role of Peter's guardian, he was 'placed in a situation he was ill-equipped for.' The barrister told the judge that, because of 'difficulties' his client had suffered during his upbringing, 'you may come to the view that the situation was a disaster waiting to happen.'

Jason Owen's barrister, Timothy Roberts QC, said that his client had not taken part in the abuse and that his crime was 'failing to report to the authorities the suspicions that he ought to have had as to how Peter was coming by his injuries.'

Mr Mendelle also read out a handwritten letter from Connelly – who had sent little notes to her defence team throughout her trials – complete with spelling and grammatical mistakes, that she had written from her Holloway cell. This was later criticised outside the court as being a self-pitying attempt on her part to win ill-deserved sympathy. The letter read:

Dear Judge,

I am writing this letter as I am not sure of a better way of expressing my regret...

I except I failed my son Peter, for which I have pleaded guilty.

By not being fully open with the social workers, I stopped them from being able to do a full job.

As a direct result of this, my son got hurt and sadly lost his short life.

I am never going to see my lovely son grow into the lovely sweet man he would have been...

I have lost all I hold dear to me. Now every day of my life is full of guilt.

I am trying to come to terms with my failure as a mother.

I punish myself on a daily basis and there is not a day that goes by where I don't cry at some point.

I have let down my family, ex-husband, myself, and most importantly my darling son.

Whilst I appreciate I am going to be given a custodial sentence I would like to say I am sorry for the pain and suffering my failure has led to.

I can only hope and pray my family, my ex-husband included, can one day forgive me for my mistakes.

However, I can never forgive myself for my shortcomings. I am truly sorry.

The next day, 22 May 2009, the trio were sentenced in Court 16 of the Old Bailey, the world's most famous criminal court. With his new partner, Peter's father sat near the dock, hanging on every word.

Wearing a raspberry-coloured top, Connelly was no doubt hoping that her last-minute pleas might have eased any sentence she was to receive. She sat, stony-faced, as Judge Stephen Kramer passed sentence.

He said: 'Any decent person who heard the catalogue of medical conditions and non-accidental injuries suffered by Peter cannot fail to have been appalled. It was clear that significant force had been used on Peter on a number of occasions.

'A child died in horrific circumstances with injuries that can only have caused great pain and distress prior to his death.'

Judge Kramer said claims by all three defendants that they knew nothing of the 'climate of abuse and neglect' in Penshurst Road 'defied belief'. He told the mother: 'You are a manipulative and self-centred person, with a calculating side as well as a temper. I reject the suggestion that you were blind to what was happening in that house or that you were naive.

'Your conduct over the months prevented Peter from being seen by Social Services. You actively deceived the authorities.

'Health professionals who saw Peter shortly before he died seem at the least to have missed the import of the injuries to him. That does not absolve you from your culpability. You acted selfishly because your priority was your relationship with Steven Barker.'

Connelly was jailed indefinitely, with at least five years in prison, while Barker received 12 years for his role in Peter's death. He was also given a life sentence with a minimum of 10 years for raping the two-year-old girl.

Jason Owen was given an indeterminate sentence for failing

to prevent the boy's death and was told that he would spend at least three years behind bars.

The only time Connelly showed any emotion was when Steven Barker was jailed for life for raping the little girl. Her mouth fell open and she mouthed the word, 'No!'

Minutes later, she returned to court with her barrister in a failed bid to make the judge reconsider the indefinite nature of the sentence passed on her. The judge had said that he would not indulge in 'judicial speculation' about who killed Peter, but said that Barker's attack on the little girl was 'abhorrent'. He then said to Barker: 'You played a major role in the events which culminated in Peter's death, you abused the position of trust you held towards a toddler. You have been found guilty of the rape of another child. This offence combines the aggravating features of a massive breach of trust and the rape of the most vulnerable of victims. You are a threat to young children.' He was put on the Sex Offenders' Register, disqualified from working with children and cannot be released until August 2017 at the earliest.

To Owen, the judge said: 'What happened to Peter in the time that you were there happened in an atmosphere that allowed a complete lack of care to be ingrained with a sickening and descending loss of personal responsibility. You were more concerned about your own situation and about the horror of what was happening to Peter being discovered than taking steps to protect him.'

The judge stressed that the three would not be automatically released once their minimum sentences expired: 'I make it clear that does not mean that you will then be automatically released. It will be for the Parole Board to determine when – or if – you are deemed no longer to be a risk to the public and in particular, children.'

Normally, prisoners are released automatically once they have served half their sentence, but inmates given life tariffs or indeterminate sentences are assessed to check if they are still a danger to the public.

In fact, Connelly and Barker could have been jailed for a maximum of 14 years for their treatment of Baby P, but the judge said that he took into account the mother's guilty plea and also the fact that Barker, the boyfriend, had no previous convictions and was of limited intelligence.

Sentence had hardly been passed, however, before the criticism began over what was perceived to be the leniency of the sentences. Because Connelly had already spent a year and 279 days in custody awaiting trial – which is taken into account as part of her sentence – this meant that she could be out by 2012. Likewise, Barker had been in custody for the same length of time and so he would be eligible to apply for parole in just over 8 years.

Michele Elliott, chief executive of Kidscape, condemned the sentences as 'appalling' and said that she believed the mother and boyfriend should never be released, adding: 'Quite frankly, I don't think the public is going to forget. For the mother to possibly be out in that short a time is incredibly distressing. It raises the question – what do you have to do to get the maximum term? You tortured and tormented a baby for its entire life and you can walk away and have a life yourself? It beggars belief. I think when people realise the depth of the depravity these people sank to and what this child went through, they will share the feeling that sentencing has to be much tougher.

'The message to people who do things like this should be, "Your life is over as well – and you are not released."'

NSPCC chief executive Andrew Flanagan said: 'We are disappointed that the minimum tariff was so low. It raises the question of how bad the abuse has to be before offenders get a longer minimum time in prison. Baby Peter suffered sustained abuse, leaving him with horrendous injuries. Two of his abusers could walk free at a time when Peter should be a schoolboy with a new world in front of him. Despicable cruelty has denied him that opportunity.'

Even Connelly's own mother remarked: 'Three years is nowhere near enough for the harm she caused. I have kept quiet for too long. She will be a dead woman walking when she comes out. People will recognise her and go for her; she will never be safe.'

As anger mounted, Justice Secretary Jack Straw was moved to defend the judge and the system of indeterminate sentences that the government had introduced. He insisted Baby P's mother would only be released if parole officials believed she was no longer a danger to children.

Mr Straw said: 'These were terrible crimes, unspeakable almost beyond words. The whole country has been deeply affected by the case of Baby Peter. It will now be the role of the prison service to monitor these offenders. The judge has been clear about the minimum terms they must serve and such decisions must be for the judiciary.

'Beyond that time they will only be released if the parole

board decides it is safe to do so. If the board thinks they are not safe to release, they will remain in custody until they are, whenever that may be.'

The *Sun* newspaper, ever active in its 'Justice for Baby P' campaign, printed a petition, which soon attracted over 100,000 signatures calling for the sentences to be reviewed. For once, they failed.

In June 2009, it was announced that Attorney General Baroness Scotland had decided against referring the sentences to the Court of Appeal. She had reviewed the case papers, the law and the relevant sentencing guidelines before deciding against referring their tariffs to the Appeal Court and said: 'It was clear to me that the judge, who had heard all of the evidence, fully appreciated the gravity of these terrible offences and took into account all of the relevant factors.'

The Attorney General, who at that time had referred around a third of the sentences she had considered as being unduly lenient to the Court of Appeal, added: 'There is no realistic prospect that the Court of Appeal would increase the sentences if I referred them.'

Although there was a massive clamour for the sentences to be 'upped', other voices pointed out that under indeterminate sentencing procedures fewer than 50 prisoners had been released on their minimum terms. Naturally this did little to assuage the hordes who understandably felt the trio had escaped lightly. And their anger increased when they learned that Connelly, who had piled on two stone in weight by binging on biscuits and chocolate behind bars, had also written a letter from prison... on how to be a good parent.

In the letter to a pen-pal, she also moaned about not having cakes and scones to eat, aching from having to do unaccustomed exercise and scalding herself with hot water while making a cup of tea. No mention is made, though, of any regret on her part over what happened to her son.

Her tips on bringing up children included advice on how to cope when kids turn on the tears to get what they want. She said: 'I think the second child always cries quicker than the first. With mine she could put the tears on within seconds. The second child learns if they nag and moan loud enough, you will step in and give them their own way.'

It was in stark contrast to the self-serving she had presented in court to the judge, in that she told of spending hours watching television while dreaming of rebuilding her life once she is released. She said: 'I love watching *Grand Designs, Relocation, A Place in the Sun*, all shows… The other day this man built a house out of tyres – it's amazing. I like to get ideas for when I get another house, how I will do it up.'

One of her most notorious acts was to smother Peter's face in chocolate to hide his bruises, yet she even had the nerve to write: 'I miss cooking cakes and all the melting chocolate to cover fruit. And fresh cream scones, oh I miss cooking so much.'

And then, astonishingly, she gave the good parenting advice when she urged 'running off a leaflet' asking parents what groups they would like to attend, adding, 'they could place them in a box and the most mentioned replys could be tried. Put up a sign saying do parents have any ideas how to help kids with homework. You could get parents talking about how they help the child, say like the best way to answer the maths questions.'

And she had one more moan: her difficulty in pursuing hobbies: 'I'm rubbish at Sudoku, no matter how I try. I am no good at reading patterns so can't make a jumper.'

The banality of it all is sickening. There is a grotesque, blackest-of-black irony to a situation where a woman such as Tracey Connelly bemoans a lack of everyday luxuries. While free, she deprived her own son of the basic right to love and care yet behind bars she seemed genuinely aggrieved at the slightest deprivation she was forced to cope with.

Connelly's actions against her son have made her a hate figure almost ranking alongside child murderer Myra Hindley in the public's gallery of most evil women in the history of British crime, but only one thing prevented her from being 'elevated' to that level. Despite mention of her name at the earliest hearings, local references to her on the streets of Tottenham and Internet naming and shaming (her defence lawyers had at one stage argued this hampered their client from receiving a fair trial), most people still did not know who she was. The same applied to Steven Barker. Much was known of him, many of his characteristics and his brutal lifestyle had been written about, but he remained anonymous. There were no pictures of the pair, no names to remember.

All that was to change soon in a dramatic manner when the world would eventually come to learn their full, revolting story.

14

NAMED & SHAMED

A S MIDNIGHT STRUCK on the night of Monday, 10 August 2009, Reuters news agency –for over 150 years famous for its immediate transmission of major news events – sent out to the world a 460-word story, which began:

> The mother of Baby P, jailed for causing or allowing her toddler son to die following a horrific campaign of domestic violence, can be officially named after the lifting of a court order on Tuesday. Tracey Connelly, 28, and her boyfriend Steven Barker, 33, were convicted last year of being responsible for the death of baby Peter in August 2007.

Finally, the evil cat was out of the bag.

The legal restrictions that kept Connelly and Barker – and therefore Peter – anonymous, no longer applied. A fresh avalanche of words and information was about to shed more light on the lives of Baby P's tormentors and their pictures too: she lifeless, dull-eyed and with her mouth slightly open as though closing it might require too much effort; he bullish and leering, with a hint of menace in his acid glare.

The reporting restrictions that had kept their names 'secret' were lifted after a ruling by a High Court judge who said it was a necessary move to maintain public confidence in the judicial system.

Mr Justice Coleridge's decision to end the anonymity of Connelly and Barker followed pressure from several major media organisations who were of the view that it was important to ensure that those who caused the toddler's death were held properly to account.

In fact, Haringey Council had attempted to keep Connelly's name secret before the Old Bailey trial the previous year. The council wanted a ban not just on the names and address of defendants Connelly and Barker, but also on the borough in which Baby Peter died. At that time, Judge Stephen Kramer indicated that in the interests of open justice the media could report that Peter died in Tottenham and also the names of the doctors and carers responsible for him.

And now Mr Justice Coleridge said the pair could be named in the interests of article 10 of the Human Rights Act, the right to freedom of expression, and in order that the public did not lose faith in the criminal justice system. He said the case was so notorious that, 'for the public to be prohibited from learning the identity of the defendants may give rise to considerable public disquiet.'

His judgement also mentioned extreme levels of vitriol aimed at the pair on the Internet, where, despite the strict order previously banning their identification, they had already been named and identified. So widespread was this that one Facebook site with 68,000 members called for them to be tortured and hanged. Discussion forums about the case of Peter continue to bring forth furious reaction.

The judge said that the case had become, 'iconic in the same way that Victoria Climbie's did,' adding, 'The level of press coverage has included a great deal of vitriol targeted at the defendants.'

Rosalind McInnes, a lecturer in media law at Glasgow University, was quoted as saying on the day that the names became officially known that the case might make it easier for the press to name adults convicted of similar offences in the future.

'When in practice some information – whether it's a name or a photograph – can be reached by millions at the press of a button, and those millions know the information is there, the law risks making itself look foolish.' She also stated that the media were now much better placed to ask for any court order to be lifted, 'where an order has been substantially undermined by publication on the Internet.'

Ms McInnes said that 'more and more judges' were trusting juries to come to a verdict based purely on the evidence given in court, disregarding anything else they might hear about the defendants: 'Where there is also a privacy dimension, as there was with Baby Peter's siblings, the balancing of the human rights involved becomes harder, but there will always come a point at which the toothpaste is out of the tube and the courts have to operate within that reality.'

The easing of restrictions meant that it was also revealed that

Jason Owen was Barker's brother and it therefore emerged, as we have already read, that the pair had tormented their late grandmother, years ago in Kent.

There were some who argued against Connelly and Barker being identified, but the majority felt otherwise. As Mr Justice Coleridge so succinctly put it: 'the boil must be lanced.' One consequence of their being named, however, was that Connelly and Barker would probably have to be given new identities when released, at a possible cost to the taxpayer of £1 million.

Under human rights laws Connelly could be granted lifelong anonymity once she was freed by claiming that she had the right to a life free from vigilante attacks or intrusion by the media, therefore she would be given a new name, moved to a home equipped with panic buttons and provided with round-the-clock police protection for the rest of her life.

Notorious crimes against children had previously resulted in protection orders for those who committed them: Mary Bell, who killed two boys when she was 11; Maxine Carr, who provided a false alibi for Ian Huntley after he murdered two Soham schoolgirls, and the schoolboy killers of toddler James Bulger.

Harry Fletcher, assistant general secretary of the probation union NAPO, said there would be ongoing consequences for the prison and probation services following the naming of Connelly and Barker: 'At some future date, if and when they are released, there will be a security issue. Like Ronnie Biggs, Connelly will be pursued by newspapers and her release date and location of her release could well be leaked in the media; this would obviously cause security issues.'

Before her release, lawyers for Connelly could apply for a 'Mary Bell order', which will give their client a new identity and anonymity if they could prove that her life was in danger.

Poor little Baby P! How could he have known the legal bonanza that his brief life was to lead to?

No sooner had the identity of his tormentors become known than yet another legal issue was raised. Days after the naming and so-called shaming of Barker, came a dramatic move on his part.

Barker, who claimed in prison that in his childhood he would be attacked by his father and hit if he answered back or did not eat his dinner, was to appeal against his life sentence for the rape of the 2-year-old. His lawyers had lodged papers calling for a hearing into his rape conviction, saying the young girl's evidence was flawed.

The papers argued on his behalf that the account was not 'competent' or 'coherent', said medical reports of her injuries were 'not supportive' of rape and insisted Barker's conviction was 'wrong and unsafe'. And they also stated that her evidence in court was 'contradictory, unintelligible and with long silences, making it impossible to cross-examine.'

Ultimately, Connelly and the Barker brothers lodged appeals against their sentences in relation to Baby P, but they were not the only ones who felt their cases should be reviewed.

Sharon Shoesmith, as we have read, was taking action over her dismissal at Haringey Council, but she was not alone in that. Her £80,000-a-year deputy Cecilia Hitchen and three other Haringey Child Protection workers, who were fired without compensation, were also appealing.

Hitchen had been sacked for 'loss of trust and confidence' after inspectors published the damning report on the children's services department that she was running with Shoesmith.

Also appealing against dismissal was social worker, Maria Ward, who had been dismissed for gross misconduct after it emerged that she saw Peter at least nine times while he was on the Child Protection Register and also failed to spot that his injuries had been covered up with chocolate. She had said that he seemed 'well' four days before he died. The General Social Work Council had also suspended her from practice.

Gillie Christou, Ms Ward's supervisor, who approved the decision to send Baby Peter back to live with his mother after her second arrest on suspicion of assaulting the child, was sacked for gross misconduct but was also appealing. She too was suspended from social work duties by the General Social Work Council, pending investigation.

Clive Preece, former head of safeguarding at Haringey, had also launched an appeal against his sacking for gross misconduct. He had played key roles in the decision to send Peter back to live with his mother instead of placing him with a foster family.

Dr Sabah Al-Zayyat – the doctor who failed to spot the broken back two days before Peter died and did not carry out a full examination because the child was 'cranky' – had also began action for unfair dismissal. Great Ormond Street issued a statement: 'We can confirm we have received notice of legal action. The trust will vigorously defend its position. We believe we acted fairly and in the interests of patients. Detailed rebuttal of Dr Al-Zayyat's claims will have to wait for any hearing. We didn't scapegoat her. The case surrounds her dismissal from GOSH following the decision not to renew her fixed-term contract.'

Then came the news of the next legal action: that Baby P's father intended to sue Haringey Council for at least £200,000 for its failure to protect his son. The total bill facing the council, and therefore its council-tax payers, could amount to well over £1.5 million and legal fees might easily outstrip that figure.

The besieged council was now under attack from all sides: a new report by Ofsted, released in mid-summer, had said vulnerable children were still at risk in the borough. Haringey had made only 'limited' progress in tackling the areas of weakness identified in the December report and although there had been some improvements, including tackling a backlog of cases, Ofsted now said that there were still concerns about the most vulnerable: 'Inspectors and the council identified serious concerns about the safety of some children named in social care files, and the council and its partners accept that currently not all children are adequately safeguarded.'

The review team said that social workers' caseloads remained too high and their decisions in individual Child Protection cases were still 'inconsistent and insufficiently robust', they found. Inspectors expressed particular concern about the recording and tracking of cases and the local authority's ability to make further improvements.

Reviews, appeals, lawyers, investigations, reports, recommendations, repercussions... on and on they went, and will no doubt continue for years to come. But away from the men and women in suits, was a vast army or ordinary men and women who read every word they could in their newspapers, switched their radios and televisions on for the latest development and shook their heads in disbelief at every revelation of error and incompetence.

The British public marched, wrote letters, composed songs, posted messages, all inspired not by fees or possible loss of their jobs, but sorrow over the loss of Baby P: so tragic, so avoidable. Some of their action was certainly helped, if not orchestrated by newspapers, but much of it was instinctive. There were memorable meetings and gatherings on his birth date and on the anniversary of his death. Proof that in a terrible world, people still cared.

But what of those who had let Baby P die? It seemed even their own parents condemned them.

Connelly's mother Mary O'Connor said her daughter could 'rot in hell'. The mother who had helped give Connelly, in her daughter's own words, a 'shitty' childhood, now said: 'I haven't got any sympathy for her at all. Maybe now she will feel fear and understand what my grandson went through as he was being tortured to death. She got off lightly with a minimum of five years. It won't be long until she's out living her life again. She sent me a visiting order, but I couldn't stand to be in the same room as her.'

And the 63-year-old father of the two Barker brothers, who understandably did not wish to be named, echoed those sentiments when he said: 'What they did was awful and they deserve to be punished. I don't care what happens to them. Everyone thinks they are monsters and I don't think any different.'

Gradually, the jailed couple's 'feelings' were becoming

known, normally through letters sent from behind bars. At one stage, Steven Barker even had the temerity to try and depict himself as a caring step-father, who would tuck the children in at night, get sandwiches ready for the next day and gently brush their hair before they set off to school with their packed lunches. As he awaited trial, he said in one statement, which only became public knowledge after he was named, that he remembered buying them Easter eggs in the spring of 2007 and – most sickeningly – 'By the time I got home from work, the kids would be in bed although the weekends they would still be up. They would wake up when I got in and I said goodnight to them.'

Finally, what of Tracey Connelly?

Tracey – the big girl whose mother had a terrible childhood, who then had a terrible childhood of her own. And then in a never-ending cycle gave her son a terrible childhood of his own. Tracey, the heavy-drinking slob, who let her only son die under her roof while she lay on a sofa and watched trash television or sat glued to Internet porn. The very embodiment of the 'me, me, me' generation, she was a woman who seemed to care just for herself, not for her own child.

Her letters from jail – after being held in Holloway, Connelly was moved to Low Newton prison, near Durham – home to, among others, Gloucester House of Horror killer Rose West – gave an insight into what passed for her 'thinking'.

Snatches of her letters are enough to make any civilised person despair. There is no regret, no promise of rehabilitation, no awareness of the piece she formed in a jigsaw from Hell. Instead – and these are various, brief excerpts – there is nothing but a stream of banal trivia centred on her own existence.

A typical line read: 'I don't plan to get attached to anyone for a very long time. Im just going to s*** about for a bit and just have loads of fun.'

'I just can't wait till this is all over so I then will know when Im getting out of this stupid place. it drives me crazy. I feel like I'm in a box.'

She even expressed a desire to be reunited with her daughters, saying: 'He [Barker] has cost me more than just my boy,' adding, 'Knowing Steven conned me is driving me nuts, how the **** I never saw through him I do not know. Somehow I will find a way to make that t***** pay.'

And in one of the sickest passages, she even told how she had contemplated suicide, but would not proceed because if her concerns for her daughters: 'As for doing something stupid, I would be lying if I said I hadn't thought about it.

'I think about it every day but I can't kill myself. I have my daughters to think about, so I have to keep fighting. Im not the sort of person to give up.'

In another letter written between court appearances, she complained: 'I'm not really sure what my hopes for the future are as coming to prison has messed up all my plans. First I'm going to use my time doing education – English, Maths and maybe Business Studies. Second I will be doing courses and stuff on my relationships, and strong therapy to help me get my head back in a good place. Third I just want to work hard and get through my time the best I can.'

Once, writing about her birthday, she said: 'I think for the first year ever I did feel my age. Funny, when I could go out I could binge-drink for England and wake up with a clear head. Yet when I stay sober, I feel like I got a bloody hangover.'

Bloated, ugly Tracey even complained about lack of sex: 'It feels like it's going to be forever till I have sex again. I've been obsessed lately about it. I need sex like a heroin addict needs a fix. I look forward to going out and I bet we will have a right laugh but be warned I'm a really friendly drunk who ends up kissing everyone!'

She added that she did not know what Barker was doing to her son in the house in Penshurst Road and hoped that he 'rotted in Hell.'

The most fascinating thing that she could find to write about was her attempts to lose weight in the prison gym: 'I can be a lazy cow when I want to be. I know when I get out I'm not going to bother with the gym. I will just buy a Wii and a Wii Fit, then I can make a fool of myself at home and no one can see.'

She asked a friend in one note: 'Do you watch Big Brother? I really love it, but this year I think they're all a bit gone in head LOL.'

Connelly – who said life would be 'one long party' when she got out – even revealed, 'I would love to visit Egypt and Greece and Rome. I would love to see the Pyramids and go down the Nile. Plus I hope to move out of London as this place has been a living hell for me since I was very little.'

And then, in one chaotic, illiterate, confused sentence she almost, but not quite, summed up her life and the world in which she and increasing numbers like her had come to live: 'I did plead guilty as after a long time thinking about everything I accept I failed as a mother for which I also accepted I would stay in prison for a number of years.'

Poor, poor Baby P. Tiny, defenceless, so achingly vulnerable in a world inhabited by monsters and with no one to really protect him. Doomed from almost the beginning, he never stood a chance.

PERSONNEL INVOLVED IN THE BABY P CASE

Baby P: Peter Connelly, born 1 March 2006, died 3 August 2007.

Tracey Connelly: Peter's mother.

Steven Barker: Peter's brutal 'step-father'.

Jason Owen: Barker's elder brother, who had changed his surname.

Mary O'Connor: Tracey Connelly's mother.

Richard Johnson: Tracey Connelly's natural father.

Sharon Shoesmith: Head of children's services at Haringey Council

Cecilia Hitchen: Shoesmith's deputy.

George Meehan: Haringey Council leader.

Liz Santry: Haringey Council's cabinet member for children and young people.

Clive Preece: Haringey Council's head of safeguarding services.

Agnes White: Social worker.

Maria Ward: Social worker.

Sylvia Henry: Social worker.

Paulette Thomas: Health visitor.

Yvonne Douglas: Health visitor.

Angela Godfrey: A family friend.

Nevres Kemal: Former Haringey social worker and whistleblower.

Gillie Christou: Team manager in council Children's Services.

Karolina Jamry: Mental health worker.

Dr Sabah Al-Zayyat: The doctor who saw Peter two days before he died.

Dr Heather Mackinnon: Consultant paediatrician concerned by Peter's injuries, who contacted Social Services.

Dr Jerome Ikwueke: GP who saw Peter several times and twice referred him to specialists after becoming concerned.

TIMETABLE OF THE LIFE OF BABY P, PETER CONNELLY, AND THE EVENTS THAT TOOK PLACE AFTER HIS DEATH

2006

1 March: Baby P, Peter Connelly, is born in hospital. His mother is Tracey Connelly.

22 March: Health visitor Yvonne Douglas makes first home visit. Peter has oral thrush.

24 March: Family GP Jerome Ikwueke sees Peter for the condition.

7 April: Yvonne Douglas weighs Peter at baby clinic.

13 April: Six-week examination by Dr Ikwueke.

2 May: A visit to the GP for diarrhoea and vomiting.

4 May: Yvonne Douglas sees mother and Baby P at health clinic.

22 May: First vaccinations for meningitis and diphtheria.

28 May: Peter is vomiting after feeds, mother calls out-of-hours emergency service.

4 June: GP visit for pain, diarrhoea and vomiting.

9 June: Tracey Connelly seen for depression by mental health worker Karolina Jamry.

19 June: GP visit, second immunisations.

11 August: Tracey Connelly sees Ms Jamry about marital problems.

15 September: Home visit by health visitor Yvonne Douglas.

19 September: Peter is seen by GP for nappy rash.

13 October: Seen by GP for bruising to head and chest. Peter's mother claims this was caused by an accidental fall downstairs.

17 November: GP visit for upper respiratory tract infection and thrush.

11 December: Peter is admitted to the Whittington Hospital in north London with bruising to his forehead and nose, sternum and right shoulder/breast.

12 December: He is examined and referred to a Child Abuse Investigation team, seen by Detective Constable Angela Slade.

13 December: Peter is examined on the ward by consultant paediatrician Heather Mackinnon.

14 December: Dr Mackinnon examines Peter on the ward.

15 December: He discharged into the care of family friend, Angela Godfrey. A police investigation begins.

18 December: Social worker Agnes White visits Tracey Connelly at home.

19 December: Peter's mother and grandmother are arrested and interviewed at Hornsey police station, north London.

21 December: Peter's leg X-rayed in hospital.

22 December: His mother attends a Child Protection conference with Haringey social workers and Dr Mackinnon. Peter is placed on the Child Protection Register.

24 December: An emergency duty team visits Angela Godfrey's home to check on Peter.

27 December: Social worker Agnes White visits Peter at Godfrey's home and returns later, unannounced.

29 December: Agnes White returns for check on Peter's contact with his mother.

2007

(Peter was returned to his mother by January. Steven Barker was living at the family home in or around this time.)

9 January: Angela Godfrey takes Peter to health clinic for thrush on buttocks and is seen by Yvonne Douglas.

12 January: Peter's leg is X-rayed again in hospital.

16 January: Agnes White checks for a second time on Peter's contact with his mother.

17 January: Peter's leg is X-rayed again in hospital.

19 January: Tracey Connelly is seen by Ms Jamry.

25 January: There is a visit to the GP for nappy rash.

26 January: Repeat visit by Agnes White to check on Peter's contact with his mother, who is seen on the same day by Ms Jamry.

2 February: Peter's third set of vaccinations and Maria Ward allocated as social worker.

8 February: Preliminary assessment of mother by (unspecified official) Caroline Sussex.

18 February: Peter and mother move to new address in Haringey: Penshurst Road, Tottenham.

22 February: Social worker Maria Ward's first home visit.

27 February: Miss Ward attends case conference at Haringey.

2 March: Miss Ward and health visitor Paulette Thomas visit Peter's mother at home.

5 March: Miss Ward questions mother after school nurse sees her slap a child.

6 March: Unannounced visit by Miss Ward.

8 March: Visit by Miss Ward.

14 March: Visit by family support service worker Marie Lockhart.

16 March: Haringey Child Protection conference with mother, attended by Miss Ward and Miss Lockhart.

20 March: Mother and P videoed at parenting class.

22 March: Visit from Miss Ward.

23 March: One-year check at health clinic.

29 March: Haringey case conference.

9 April: Peter seen by GP with bruising to face. Tracey Connelly claims he was pushed into a fireplace by another child. Peter is admitted to North Middlesex Hospital for bruising and swelling to the head.

10 April: Peter is referred to child development clinic by a social worker who sees him 'head-banging'.

11 April: Peter is discharged from North Middlesex Hospital.

12 April: Child Protection meeting at North Middlesex.

24 April: Home visit by Miss Ward.

3 May: Tracey Connelly and Peter attend parenting class.

9 May: Planned home visit by health visitor, Ms Thomas.

16 May: Family support visit by Ms Lockhart.

18 May: GP visit for hives, an allergic reaction.

21 May: Miss Ward visits.

(In or around June, Jason Owen, Barker's elder brother, moves in with his 15-year-old girlfriend and his children.)

1 June: Miss Ward makes an unannounced visit and reports

Peter's mother to police over bruises to her child, who is taken to North Middlesex Hospital for a check-up.

5 June: Mother interviewed under caution at Hornsey police station.

6 June: Peter is seen by Ms Thomas at the health clinic.

7 June: More immunisations at GP surgery and Child Protection meeting at North Middlesex Hospital.

8 June: Police take photos of Peter and seize a toy from his home.

12 June: Registered childminder Anne Walker takes Peter for day care for 10 days.

15 June: Home visit by Ms Lockhart.

19 June: Miss Ward visits childminder.

20 June: Case conference at Haringey.

21 June: Peter and his mother attend a parenting class.

5 July: Peter and his mother attend another parenting class.

9 July: Mother takes Peter to North Middlesex Hospital with an ear infection.

11 July: Home visit by Miss Ward.

18 July: Peter is seen at a health clinic for a scalp and ear infection.

19 July: Tracey Connelly and Peter attend a parenting class and attend North Middlesex Hospital concerning the infection.

26 July: GP visit for head lice and blood in Peter's ear.

30 July: Case conference at Haringey. Home visit by Miss Ward when chocolate was smeared on Peter's face to hide bruises. Tracey Connelly is feeling stressed.

31 July: Police hand reports to Crown Prosecution Service, including statements from two doctors saying that Peter's bruising suggested 'non-accidental' injury. Prosecutors decide there is insufficient evidence to bring a case.

1 August: Peter seen at St Ann's Hospital in north London by locum paediatrician Sabah Al-Zayyat. She decides that she cannot carry out a full check-up – the boy is 'cranky'. The post-mortem later reveals he had probably suffered a broken back and fractured ribs at this stage.

2 August: Tracey Connelly is told police will take no further action over assault allegations.

3 August: At 11.36am there is a 999 call from Peter's home. 11.40am the ambulance arrives. 11.43am ambulance leaves. 11.49am ambulance arrives at hospital. 12.10pm Peter is pronounced dead and police are called. 13.30pm Body maps complete. 13.45pm Tracey Connelly is arrested.

(November 2007: Tracey Connelly and Steven Barker appear in court to deny murder and allowing or failing to prevent Peter's death. Jason Owen denies allowing or failing to prevent his death. At this stage all three were named. Connelly and Barker were remanded in custody, Owen was granted bail.

2008

11 November: Connelly and Barker (now not named) and Jason Owen are cleared of murder. She pleads guilty and they are found guilty of causing or allowing Peter's death.

12 November: Children's secretary Ed Balls orders an urgent review of Haringey Council's Children's Welfare Services.

14 November: It is revealed that former Haringey social worker Nevres Kemal wrote to the government six months before Peter died, expressing concern over Child Protection services in the area. Ministers did not investigate further, saying it was

a matter for the Commission for Social Care Inspection (CSCI).

21 November: The General Medical Council suspends Dr Sabah Al-Zayyat's registration as a doctor.

26 November: Prime Minister Gordon Brown is handed a newspaper petition with more than 1 million signatures calling for the social workers involved in the Baby P case to be sacked.

1 December: Ed Balls describes the findings of a report into Haringey Children's Services as 'devastating'. Haringey Council's leader George Meehan and cabinet member for children and young people Liz Santry resign. Sharon Shoesmith is removed as the local authority's director of children's services by Mr Balls, but she remains suspended on full pay.

8 December: Shoesmith is sacked with immediate effect by a panel of councillors and told she will not receive any compensation.

12 December: It is announced that Shoesmith's replacement will be Peter Lewis from Enfield.

2009

6 January: Ms Shoesmith is to appeal against her dismissal.

12 January: A panel of Haringey councillors rejects Shoesmith's appeal.

26 January: The government appoints a social work taskforce to carry out a comprehensive review of social services in Britain.

6 February: Shoesmith condemns the political handling of the Baby P case as 'breathtakingly reckless' and admits she

contemplated suicide in interviews with the *Guardian* and Radio 4's *Woman's Hour*.

17 February: The General Medical Council suspends from practice family GP Dr Jerome Ikwueke, who, on two occasions referred Peter to hospital specialists after becoming concerned about suspicious marks on his face and body.

6 March: Shoesmith lodges an employment tribunal claim for unfair dismissal against Haringey Council and also launches an application for judicial review against the council, Mr Balls and Ofsted. She is also to claim sex discrimination.

12 March: A review of Child Protection in Britain by Lord Laming finds that too many authorities have failed to adopt reforms introduced following the death of 8-year-old Victoria Climbie in Haringey. The new review was ordered after Peter's death.

30 April: Haringey sacks 4 key social workers: deputy director of children and families Cecilia Hitchen, social worker Maria Ward, team manager Gillie Christou and head of safeguarding services Clive Preece. Later, all four announce they will appeal.

1 May: Steven Barker is found guilty of raping a 2-year-old girl on Haringey Council's at-risk register. Tracey Connelly is cleared of cruelty to the girl.

22 May: Tracey Connelly is given an indeterminate sentence and told that she will have to serve a minimum of 5 years for causing or allowing her son's death before being eligible for parole. Steven Barker is sentenced to 12 years for his part in Peter's death and life for raping the 2-year-old. He must serve a minimum of 10 years, but can apply for parole after 8. Jason Owen is jailed indefinitely, but must serve at least 3 years.

There is anger over the 'lenient' sentences and the fact that the trio could soon be free.

11 August: At midnight the restrictions on naming Tracey Connelly and Steven Barker are lifted. Already, they have been named on the Internet. Soon after, it is revealed that Peter's natural father is to sue Haringey for not protecting the child.